Shut In and Win

Twenty-First Century Guidelines for a Prayer and Fasting Revival

Mamie Sconiers Leonard

Shut In and Win
Twenty-First Century Guidelines for a Prayer
and Fasting Revival
by Mamie Sconiers Leonard

Printed in the United States of America

ISBN 978-1-60647-856-1

Mamie Leonard Ministries
P.O. Box 431755
Los Angeles, CA USA 90043
(310) 330-4800 phone
(310) 330-4804 fax

info@mamieleonardshutin.org
www.mamieleonardshutin.org

www.xulonpress.com

Praise for the book...

A veteran praying and fasting warrior, Evangelist Leonard presents practical guidelines for conducting and participating in a shut-in revival. The powerful testimonies included in the book affirm the power of the Sixty-Hour Consecration unfolded in her vision from God. All believers are challenged to go deeper in their walk with the Lord through this waning spiritual discipline. This is a must-read and a must-do.

Bishop George D. McKinney, Jr.
General Board Member
Church of God in Christ, Inc.

This book should be in the hands of every believer who desires more intimacy with the Lord. Fasting and praying are foundational to our spiritual development. How much more effective we are when we join together to pull down the strongholds of the enemy so that the captives can be set free. Well done, Evangelist Leonard!

Mother Willie Mae Rivers
General Supervisor
Department of Women
Church of God in Christ, Inc.

This writing profiles the journey of a surrendered vessel with the resolve to live a consecrated life. Evangelist Leonard communicates a model for an effective individual or corporate shut-in. She succinctly outlines a "how to" of prayer, fasting and Bible study for individuals seeking increased levels of God's power.

Dr. Barbara McCoo Lewis
Supervisor of Women
Southern California First Jurisdiction
Church of God in Christ, Inc.

The Mamie Leonard Shut-In Ministry has enriched my church and life. The Spirit of the Lord came into our midst, saved, healed, and delivered many. I have seen growth and development in my congregation, along with a deeper commitment to prayer. This is a ministry for the end time and should be embraced wholeheartedly.

Bishop Gregory L. Dixon
First Church of God
Inglewood, CA

Encouragement to fast and pray has never been more needed in our state of California as well as the nation. This book is a helpful tool to ignite your heart and your church's.

Dr. James Garlow
Senior Pastor Skyline Wesleyan Church
San Diego, CA

The Mamie Leonard Shut-In Ministry provided for our church a lifetime of change in accountability with God. It changed the landscape of our ministry, as well as our prayer ministry. What a timely book.

Dr. Tony Williams
Senior Pastor
Maranatha Christian Center
San Jose, CA

Mobilizing and equipping people to fast and pray for breakthrough have been a hallmark of the shut-in ministry of Mamie Leonard, along with her twin sister Martha Featherston of Interfaith Prayer Fellowship. What they have taught and learned will not be lost. This book captures the essence of what God wants to release to the broader body of Christ.

Judy Garlow Wade
Author, *Take The Name of Jesus With You*
San Diego, CA

I thank God for you and your ministry. Your visits to Cedar Grove Baptist Church were by divine appointment. Your prayers and prophecies have been one of the vehicles that ushered me into expanding within my vision, with a burning passion to do the work of the church, transcending the four walls to reach all humanity.

Elder A.T. Williams, Jr., Pastor
Cedar Grove Baptist Church
Los Angeles, CA

We are thankful to God that through the Holy Spirit he has inspired Sis. Leonard to write this book for us to learn to use her God-given gift of prayer and fasting, so that we may learn to hold shut-ins. Every Christian leader needs this book to keep our followers always in an excellent relationship with the God we serve.

Rev. Howard E. Haggler
Presiding Elder
AME Zion Church
San Diego District
San Diego, CA

This power-packed and anointed book will ignite and revolutionize the Pentecostal-apostolic power in your church, your ministry, and your life as you read the first-hand accounts of signs, wonders, healings, and miracles similar to those experienced by the early church.

Bishop Johnny J. Young, Ph.D.
Senior Presiding Prelate
The Church of God Pentecostal, Inc.
Southwestern Diocese

Shut In and Win encourages the kind of deep, soul-searching and continuous devotions that led to the early and latter day outpourings of the Holy Spirit. Read it and be blessed!

Pastor Maynard Weisbrod
Senior Pastor
Calvary Evangelistic Center
Tucson, AZ

Dedication

This book is dedicated to my loving family: my late husband Pastor Alvin Leonard and my sons, Elder Mark Leonard and Minister Timothy Leonard.

Pastor Alvin Leonard went home to be with the Lord on December 28, 2007. His personal support for the shut-in ministry was unsurpassed. He humbly served in whatever capacity necessary. He traveled with the team and captured numerous key ministry moments with his video camera. He was a man of prayer and we miss him dearly. We know that he is a part of that great cloud of witnesses in heaven cheering us on to victory.

My son Mark succeeded his father as senior pastor of our church, Greater Deliverance Church of God in Christ in Inglewood, CA. My son Timothy is our co-pastor of the youth department, a praise team leader, and musician coordinator. I bless God for their faithful service in word, in song, in administration, and other areas of service in our church and shut-in ministries.

Contents

Acknowledgements

E very successful endeavor requires teamwork. I want
to thank the team that helped me to bring this book to
fruition:

Naomi Bradley, for assisting me in birthing this book
and her subsequent editing of the final manuscript; my
nephew, Navy Chaplain Charles E. Wilson, for his research
and invaluable input. The late Evangelist Kathryn Snelson
assisted in the initial editing of the first draft of the book.
Bernadette Baskerville collected the various testimonies
that appear herein and Stephanye Dillard faithfully typed
the preliminary manuscript. Lynnette Howard spent countless hours assisting me in compiling key information. Pastor
Ruby Robinson, Elvestine Evans, Doris Owens, De Shaune
Lockett, Lois Moore, and many others lent their support
to this project in innumerable ways. Best-selling Christian
author Deborah Pegues coached me in the final stages and
saw this book to completion.

Of course, there would be no story to tell without the
support team that has labored with me in various aspects
of the shut-in ministry. Their sacrifice, dedication and hard
work have provided a solid foundation for the ministry.
I'm eternally grateful to my twin sister, Evangelist Martha
Featherston (our vice president), for her role in heading the
Jericho March, the Prayer of Confession, and the Friday Night

Circle Prayer segments of the shut-ins. I owe a special debt of gratitude to her husband, Deacon Kenneth Featherston, for his work in coordinating the team in our travels and for leading the Prayer Walk and Scripture Search segments of the shut-in services. He also serves as the ministry treasurer.

Kathy Stewart deserves special commendation for her faithful participation in the Prayer Walk segment and for her efforts in consistently bringing many souls to the shut-in services. Beverly Winston designed our ministry logo and served faithfully as our secretary for several years. Pastor Lenonda Robinson, our current administrative assistant, brings a special spirit of excellence to this work. Lucille Lee and Ann Langston, coordinators of the Corporate Prayer, were filled with the Holy Ghost in this ministry over 23 years ago. They have not wavered in their role as loyal and faithful intercessors and prayer warriors; their presence and input have been invaluable.

Finally, the 9 a.m. Prayer Team at my home church, Greater Deliverance Church of God in Christ in Inglewood, CA, has consistently supported the shut-in ministry with their prayers and presence—and for that I am extremely grateful.

Prologue

It is with great pleasure that I submit to you this long-awaited "how-to" book on conducting and experiencing a prayer and fasting shut-in—the spiritual discipline of shutting inside a church together with other believers to seek the face of the Lord while humbling our souls with prayer and fasting. This practice was the norm after the great Azusa Street Revival of 1906 in the United States, where hundreds of churches, fellowships and denominations from the holiness tradition witnessed the outpouring of the Holy Ghost in the Pentecostal movement. Shut-ins were often held in private homes and in churches.

As our nation was in need of a spiritual renewal during such turbulent world events entering the twentieth century, many churches rekindled the practice of praying, fasting and shutting in the house of the Lord as a means of experiencing a deeper relationship and walk with Christ. At the turn of the 20th century, Bishop Charles Harrison Mason, founder of the Church of God in Christ, International, currently one of the largest Pentecostal denominations in the world, implemented national praying and fasting days on Tuesdays and Fridays for COGIC congregations. Intimacy with the Father was the primary objective; power and deliverance were an outgrowth of a close relationship with him. God has honored my life and allowed me to carry forth the essential tradition of calling his people to fast and pray.

The Mamie Leonard Shut-In Ministry uses a format of sixty hours (from midnight Wednesday to Saturday at noon) in fasting and prayer. Those who cannot stay full-time in the church from Thursday at 9 p.m. to noon on Saturday can come at any hour of prayer, or at the start of any other scheduled activity. However, we encourage everyone who can to stay in the church the entire time to gain the full impact.

In the following pages, we will explore the importance of a shut-in and get a clear perspective on the purpose and power of corporate praying and fasting. We will review the step-by-step guidelines and agenda for a Sixty-Hour Consecration with a community of believers. I will also give you a glimpse of the journey that brought me to the point where God called me to the shut-in ministry. You will walk with me through the obedience to the call in 1983, the vision that God gave to me in 1984 to enter a seven-year covenant of prayer and fasting shut-in revivals, and the results of my saying "Yes" to his call.

Finally, your hearts will be warmed and inspired by the powerful healing and deliverance testimonies of individuals who experienced a move of God in the shut-ins, and by the testimonies from the numerous churches that have hosted the shut-in team.

Mamie Sconiers Leonard
November 2008

Chapter 1

The Making of a Maid Servant

On January 11, 1954, I was sitting at my work station when suddenly a Divine presence overshadowed me. I began to weep uncontrollably. "Martha, I'm getting ready to tell the supervisor that I'm going home," I announced to my 22-year-old twin sister. "What's wrong?" she asked. "I don't know. I feel compelled to go and shut in the church and pray." She looked at me as if I had lost my mind. "You can't do that, Mamie!"

My sister could tell from the look on my face that her protests were falling on deaf ears. My mind was made up. Nevertheless, she continued to plead with me. "Mamie, it's too cold to stay in the church." She was almost in tears; winters in Newark, NJ were no joke. I informed the supervisor that I was leaving and promptly headed to the apartment that Martha and I shared. I needed to pack a small bag for my stay at the church.

Martha and I had enjoyed a close relationship since our birth on July 18, 1932 in Bellwood, AL. My parents, Ruben and Avie Sconiers, had moved to Panama City, FL with our four siblings (William, Hazel, Lois and Ruben, Jr.) during our early childhood. Our home was the center of hospitality. We hosted Bishop Charles Harrison Mason, founder of the

Church of God in Christ (COGIC), International, which today is one of the largest Pentecostal denominations in the world with more than seven million members. We also hosted COGIC state bishops, state supervisors, evangelists, and other saints barred by the Jim Crow laws of the South from staying in local hotels.

When Martha and I graduated from high school, my father decided that building a local COGIC church for the community was his top priority. Though he had no ambition of becoming a pastor, his passion to see a COGIC church in our community had driven his decision. Needless to say, college would be out of the question for Martha and me since all his funds would be invested in the building project. When finished, he planned to call Bishop W.R. Nesbitt, Sr., the presiding state bishop of Western Florida Jurisdiction, and ask him to appoint a pastor for the assembly that he had already organized and had begun to teach. He did just that. The church was called the Antioch Temple COGIC and remains a thriving church today. It was years before I overcame my resentment over his decision to prioritize the church over our education.

After our high school graduation, Martha and I moved to Newark, NJ where our cousin, Irene Tindell, helped us to get established in our own apartment. Our older brother had also migrated to Newark, so the presence of family made the transition a lot easier than it would have been otherwise. We immediately enrolled in night classes in a nurses' training program. We worked full-time by day in a local factory. We were blessed and thrilled to find jobs at the same company. Now it seemed that God was about to change my plans.

Called Aside for His Glory

When I arrived at the apartment, the Holy Spirit directed me to the items to include in my overnight bag for my fasting and prayer assignment at the church. I obediently packed my Bible, my tithes, a few toiletries, and a small towel. I walked the entire estimated two-mile journey to the church. Each step was a burden. I cried out to God the whole time saying, "Lord, what is it?" I felt as if I carried the weight of the world on my shoulders. I didn't even know if I would be able to get into the church.

The pastor, who lived next door to the church, was standing outside at the church entrance when I arrived. I walked up to him with tears in my eyes. He greeted me warmly, asking, "What is it? What's wrong?" I told him that the Lord had led me to come to the church. He opened the doors for me to enter. I fell at the altar. The hand of God was upon me. After some time, I opened the scriptures desperately searching for an explanation of what God was doing in me. Later that evening, the congregation gathered for the regular Tuesday night Bible study.

Martha had already called our cousin Irene and informed her of my resolve to stay in the church. After the benediction, I sat back down. Martha urged me to go home because of the cold weather and the inherent dangers of a young woman staying in the church alone. The pastor agreed. "I don't think that's a good idea for you to stay," he advised. He insisted that I leave. I responded, "It is better to obey God than man" (based upon Acts 5:29). Reluctantly, he let me remain in the church.

I admit that I was surprised at my own bravery. You see, I had always had a morbid fear of dead people and I was keenly aware that a funeral had been recently held in the church. Notwithstanding, I was overshadowed with supernatural courage and did not succumb to fear of staying in the church. Several of the people, including Martha, who had come to the service decided to spend the night with me. The pastor made his office available to me so that I could have private time with God. While God was dealing with me, he would give me a scripture. I would then close my eyes and he would give me clear revelation of its meaning and application. This took place throughout the night. In my spirit, I felt God saying to me, "You want to be a nurse, but I'm calling you to be a nurse for the sin-sick souls of people." That night, God gave me a word of knowledge or a word of prophesy for every person who came into the office.

Physically, I fared well. I did not drink any water; this was by divine mandate. The Lord instructed me to fold the small towel I had packed into a "trinity fold"—one for the Father, Son, and Holy Ghost. The hunger and thirst would dissipate when I would place the wet towel on my forehead. We know today that it is wise to flush the kidneys with lots of water when fasting; however, when you are under a divine order, God protects your system just as he did when he called Moses to a forty-day fast without water.

I lost sight of everything. Revelations abounded. It was such a glorious experience as God manifested his presence. Many of the members came to stay and pray with me in the ensuing days and nights—some out of curiosity, others out of a desire to embrace what God was doing. I had never shut in for three days and nights up to this point in my spiritual walk. I had fasted for three days and nights, but not overnight in a church. I was more accustomed to the one-night shut-ins. I was also aware of but had never attended Bishop Mason's annual three-day shut-ins in Memphis, TN to mark the beginning of COGIC's Holy Convocation.

Caught Up

On Friday night, at the conclusion of our regular weekly service, I asked the pastor if I could have words. At that time, I didn't know that the Spirit of the Lord was about to come upon me in a way I had never experienced before. With my pastor's approval, I stepped forward on the altar and stood before the audience of about 30 people. I didn't know what I would say or do. God had prompted me to move forward and I obeyed. When I did, the Spirit of the Lord came upon me so heavily that I felt surrounded by his glory. God urged me to speak. "Jesus is coming tonight!" I exclaimed. My cousin Irene protested, "Mamie, don't say that. Nobody knows when Jesus is coming!"

I didn't care what anyone said at that moment. When the power of God comes upon you like that, nothing else matters. You know God is real and want to obey his every word, without question. The Lord then unctioned me to ask two brothers in the audience to come and stand beside me. As they came forward, I began to collapse under the power of the God. The brothers arrived just in time to catch me.

I immediately went into a trance-like state, much like Peter must have experienced in Acts 10:10-11, "And he became very hungry, and would have eaten; but while they made ready, he fell into a trance, And saw heaven opened…"

I have no recollection of what happened in the natural realm after that. I saw a vision of the coming of Jesus Christ. The sky seemed as if it was on fire. It seemed as if millions were coming to God and crying for another chance. I heard the voice of the Lord telling them that it was too late. He said, "I gave you the opportunity to come and you refused."

Martha later recounted that they took me home, gave me a light meal, and put me to bed.

For three weeks, I had vision after vision. I saw Bishop Mason leading a line of saints dressed in white in a great march to heaven. They were rejoicing and singing "How I got over. My soul looks back and wonders how I got over." —a very popular song of the day. I also had a vision of hell. Its terror was beyond description. The heat was unbearable. People were screaming and pleading with God to give them another chance. His only response was, "Too late, too late."

21

According to Martha, I had limited conversations with others during this period of my trance-like state. My brother, in desperation, finally declared, "I'm going to call the doctor." Martha said at that very moment, I came out of the trance. My mother was there; she had come all the way from Panama City to see about me. I was happy to see her, but I was disappointed to be back on this earth. It was so wonderful where I was with Jesus.

The following Sunday, Martha insisted that mother keep me home from church. However, as soon as Martha left, mother told me to get dressed. We went to our church. I asked the pastor if I could have words. When I started to speak, the glory of God filled the place. He reconfirmed his call, "I've called you to be a nurse for the sin-sick souls of people." God used me in a supernatural way and many were set free. Our cousin Irene exclaimed to Martha, "There's nothing wrong with Mamie." She then went forth in a dance before God.

Notwithstanding, my mother took me back home with her to Florida. The events at my church were the beginning of my ministry 54 years ago in 1954.

Revival Time

The first Sunday after I arrived back in Panama City with my mother, I started giving my testimony and ministering in the church. I felt led to go to the junior high school located within walking distance of our home. When I arrived, I asked the principal if I could address the student body. He called a general assembly and gave me an opportunity to share my experience regarding how I wanted to be a nurse but how God had called me to be a nurse for the sin-sick souls of people. The students listened with rapt attention.

We lived in a small country town outside of Panama City. It wasn't long before word spread about what God was doing in my life—and the miraculous signs that followed. People would come out of their houses and onto the porch when they heard I was coming down the street. Some came merely to see how I was behaving in light of the fact that they had heard that I had lost my mind. However, when they saw the power of God in my life, they looked forward to hearing a word from the Lord.

I'll never forget our 40-year-old neighbor, Margie. The Lord gave me a word of knowledge for her one day when she was visiting our home: "It's time to give your life to the Lord or something terrible will happen to you." Margie was sitting in our dining room chair at that time. At my words, the Spirit of the Lord came upon her, she threw her arms up and went back in the chair and broke it in two. She avoided me for a short time after that. She ignored the voice of God. She became pregnant, but it was a tubal pregnancy that threatened her life. She lost that child. While in the hospital, she suffered a stroke, which affected her speech. Some time later, she gave her life to God and served him faithfully until her demise; however, her speech was never fully restored.

Later that year, I started traveling to various speaking engagements with Mother Susie Johnson, the Church of God in Christ state supervisor for Western Florida. I also accompanied my pastor R. L. McCloud and his wife, and other evangelists on their revival circuits. They would give me the opportunity to minister in their services. I was happy to serve in the kingdom in whatever capacity needed. I even helped Elder and Sis. Joe Smith build a "paper church" in Marianna, FL consisting of heavy butcher paper attached to six-foot wooden stakes. We constructed it to define our space on a vacant lot where we conducted a revival. It held up for about a week before the natural elements prevailed against its flimsy construction. Notwithstanding, the people came out for the revival. They were hungry for God and Pentecostalism was still relatively young in the area.

In 1957, Martha met the love of her life, Kenneth Featherston. Their pastor, Bishop J.A. Blake, Sr. in San Diego, CA, united the couple in holy matrimony in July 1958. (They celebrated their fiftieth wedding anniversary in grand style in July 2008.) It would be another six years before I would marry the man whom God had chosen to be my life partner.

Alvin Leonard

I began to get requests to conduct youth revivals and to address the youth at COGIC conferences. One year, when I was participating in an open forum at the International Youth Congress in Miami, FL, Alvin Leonard spotted me and resolved on the spot that I would be his wife. Of course, he didn't say a word to me and I was totally unaware of his affections—and his existence! During my evangelistic travels, I made several trips to the Southern California area where I spent time with my younger sister Lois and her husband Robert Salter. I would also attend services with Martha and Kenneth at Bishop J.A. Blake, Sr.'s Greater Jackson Memorial COGIC in San Diego. One particular Sunday, Bishop Blake announced that since I was such a frequent visitor he was going to take me in as a regular member. I submitted and he became my official pastor.

One evening in 1962, while visiting my friend Johnnie Mae Williams in Los Angeles, I attended a state choir rehearsal. Afterwards, Alvin Leonard came to pick up his cousin, Shirley Gissendanner, who sang in the choir. She had expressed to me on several occasions that she desired to introduce us. I learned that, ironically, he was also an identical twin. I also learned that he was a faithful man of God, having been mentored spiritually and vocationally by his pastor Elder Clarence E. Church, Sr.

Alvin co-labored with Elder Church to build the first permanent worship facility for the West Angeles COGIC on Adams Boulevard in Los Angeles, CA in 1955. After Elder Church's death in 1968, Elder Charles Blake, son of Bishop J.A. Blake, Sr., was appointed pastor in 1969. Under his leadership, the church experienced phenomenal growth, which required the congregation to make two subsequent moves to larger facilities, including the now world famous West Angeles Cathedral. With a membership of over 20,000, the church has been recognized as one of the fastest growing churches in the nation. Bishop Charles Blake is currently the presiding bishop of the Church of God in Christ, International. Alvin was honored to have played an integral part in Bishop Blake's journey at West Angeles.

Alvin and I had pursued our long distance relationship for approximately two years before he proposed. I immediately informed him that my doctors had advised me that I would not be able to bear children due to fibroid tumors. "I'm not marrying you to have children. I'm marrying you because I love you." With that settled, we were married on June 27, 1964 by Bishop J.A. Blake, Sr. and Elder Clarence Church, Sr. God showed Himself strong and allowed me to conceive and deliver two miracle boys—Timothy Earl in 1965 and Mark Eleazer in 1968.

During the 70s, Alvin and I pursued our call to ministry. In 1974, he was ordained as an elder and appointed assistant pastor of the Mt. Calvary COGIC, where he served for fifteen years before God called him to head his own pastoral ministry in 1986. He served as the loving pastor of the Greater Deliverance COGIC until his demise on December 28, 2007. God blessed us with forty-three glorious years of holy matrimony. If I had to live my life over, I wouldn't change a thing–he would still be the love of my life.

Chapter 2

The Seven-Year Covenant

In August 1983, our pastor, Elder Clarence E. Church, Jr.
asked me to conduct a revival at Mt. Calvary COGIC in
Los Angeles, CA. I was very reluctant to accept his invitation because I had already enrolled in college. You see, I was
51 years old and finally had opportunity to pursue my formal
education. I wanted to become a counselor. Nevertheless, I
agreed to conduct a one-week revival. I sought assistance
from Elder Ronald C. Hill, pastor at Love and Unity COGIC
in Compton, CA.

Immediately, the Lord placed an urgent desire within me
to seek him through fasting and praying. I shared this with
Elder Hill and we agreed to begin the revival with a three-
day shut-in. On the second day of the shut-in while travailing
in the noon prayer, God spoke to my spirit in a miraculous
way. He said, "I have found favor in you and I can trust you
with a ministry of deliverance." He revealed to me that the
shut-in ministry would be one of the ministries that would
bring the body of Christ together and restore spiritual gifts
to the church.

During the one-week revival, the Lord gave me specific
instructions regarding how he would prepare me for ministry.
My daily curriculum was to consist of one hour of prayer and

three hours of study of the word. He also gave specific direction for the shut-in ministry. The ministry was to consist of three days of praying and fasting each month for the next six months. Those who would join me were to begin fasting on Wednesday at midnight in their homes, come into the church facility on Thursday night at 9 p.m. and remain there until Saturday at noon. This would be a total of sixty hours of consecration.

I heard the voice of God clearly; however, I thought I could compromise with him by fasting and praying in my home while pursuing my education. This most assuredly was not in alignment with God's plan. The Lord said, "Mamie, I want you in the church full-time and not at home." His stern rebuke created a spiritual struggle within. I would have to radically alter my personal plans and obey the voice of God completely. This internal struggle lasted a week. I felt frustrated, hurt, and rejected by God. I said to him, "I could do a better job for you if I could complete my education." I wondered why God allowed others to complete their education but would not give me the same privilege.

It was during my internal struggle that the Lord spoke clearly and audibly into my spirit. He said, "It is not you doing the work, it is I working through you. Your schooling will consist of studying my word three hours, and praying one hour daily. You are just a vessel to be used by me." The Lord continued to speak to me from the scriptures.

"What? Know ye not that your body is the temple of the Holy Ghost which is in you, which ye have of God, and ye are not your own? For ye are bought with a price: therefore glorify God in your body, and in your spirit, which are God's" (1 Corinthians 6:19-20).

And,

"Before I formed thee in the belly I knew thee; and before thou camest forth out of the womb I sanctified thee, and I ordained thee a prophet unto the nations" (Jeremiah 1:5).

Through these scriptures the revelation of God was illuminated in my spirit. He assured me that he had called and chosen me from birth. The calling for my life included God's plan for the shut-in ministry.

The three-day shut-in would symbolize the death, burial, and resurrection of Jesus Christ. The first day, we die to sin. The second day we are buried with Christ. The third day we are resurrected a new creature in Christ Jesus. As I began to obey God's plan for the shut-in, I became more aware of how the power of God plays a part in the life of the believer.

In the beginning of the shut-ins, we encountered unclean spirits over which we did not possess power. However, we applied Jesus' principles laid out in Matthew 17:21: "Howbeit this kind goeth not out but by prayer and fasting." We began to see miraculous deliverance through the power of God. (See chapters 10 and 11 for testimonies of various breakthroughs.)

Upon completion of the six months, God let me know that this was not the end of the shut-in ministry. He used my twin sister, Martha, to usher in the next phase. In April 1984, the Interfaith Prayer Fellowship, which Martha had founded in San Diego, CA, invited me to conduct a shut-in in that city as part of Martha's installation service as president of the organization. On this glorious, unforgettable occasion, women and men from 34 churches representing Baptists, Lutherans, Catholics, Methodists, Pentecostals, Presbyterians, and Seventh-Day Adventists participated in the services.

God placed his stamp of approval on both the shut-in ministry and the Interfaith Prayer Fellowship by healing, saving, delivering, filling with the Holy Ghost, and inspiring hundreds that attended from all over Southern California. It was a spiritual gathering similar to the day of Pentecost when God poured out his Spirit upon all that waited in the upper room. As a result of that meeting, invitations to conduct shut-in revivals poured in. Just as God blessed the Interfaith Prayer Fellowship to be inter-denominational, he also blessed the Mamie Leonard Shut-In Ministry to be embraced in like manner.

God then unfolded his plan for the next phase of the shut-in ministry. It was to continue for seven years! He spoke these words to my heart:

> *"Mamie, if you will go among my people for seven years and be obedient to my instruction, then you will see the glory of God being manifested in your presence. You will see the eyes of the blind opened, deaf ears unstopped, the lame walk, body limbs restored, and drug addicts and other abusers set totally free. You will see spiritual gifts and the ministry of deliverance in full operation. You will experience a great revival."*

To seal my commitment, I entered into a divine covenant with the Lord.

It was during this seven-year covenant period that the motto and theme of the shut-in ministry were developed: "Say It, Believe It, and Receive It! Shut In and Win." This motto was based upon Mark 11:23: "For verily I say unto you, that whosoever shall say unto this mountain, be thou removed, and be thou cast into the sea; and shall not doubt in his heart, but shall believe that those things which he saith shall come to pass; he shall have whatsoever he saith."

Our theme is a reminder of our commitment: "My covenant will I not break, nor alter the thing that is gone out of my lips" (Psalms 89:34).

The first shut-in in 1983 at Mt. Calvary in Los Angeles began with nineteen people. Only four spent the entire time in the church, including myself and Elder Ron Hill, who had joined me in conducting the shut-ins. Pastors from many denominations across the United States would soon open their churches for us to come in and conduct a shut-in revival. After the seven-year covenant ended in 1991, God spoke and said, "You have finished, but I have not finished with you." The shut-ins were to continue on a God-directed schedule.

The Lord has blessed and expanded the ministry with five staff members, many team members, and a host of followers who have traveled with us from coast to coast in the United States and Jamaica. Since inception, we have seen as many as 1,500 people in a single shut-in.

We have conducted shut-in revivals only at the invitation of a host church. God has given us favor and we have never had to solicit a pastor to invite us to come. I have learned so much over the years regarding financial responsibility and accountability in dealing with churches. I've come to understand that in order for one to continue to see the favor and blessings of God in his personal life and the life of his ministry, he cannot have a heart greedy after money—"filthy lucre"—as described in 1 Peter 5:2. Therefore, in all these years, I have never asked a single host church for any money whatsoever as a prerequisite for us to bring our team in and conduct a shut-in revival. The Lord spoke to me and told me to go into his vineyard and work and whatsoever is right he said he will pay (Matthew 20:4). God has been faithful to His word. The freewill offerings of the people have been sufficient and the ministry has never lacked financially.

It has been over twenty-five years that we have witnessed the mighty move of God in the shut-in ministry. We have seen thousands of souls come to Christ, countless people filled with the Holy Ghost, marriages restored, miraculous healings of cataracts, brain tumors, cancers, diabetes, arthritis, heart conditions, sickle cell, and other physical conditions. There has been an untold number of Christians that have made new commitments to God and have gone on to bless others through their new fervor for Christ.

Chapter 3

What is a Shut-In?

A shut-in is coming aside to seek the Lord through prayer and fasting in the house of the Lord. A good example of this is found in 2 Chronicles 20:3-5:

> "And Jehoshaphat feared, and set himself to seek the LORD, and proclaimed a fast throughout all Judah. And Judah gathered themselves together, to ask help of the LORD: even out of all the cities of Judah they came to seek the LORD. And Jehoshaphat stood in the congregation of Judah and Jerusalem, in the house of the LORD, before the new court...."

Like the word "rapture," the term "shut-in" is not found in the Bible. But the practice of coming aside for a time of prayer and fasting is found throughout the Old and New Testaments:

> "Gird yourselves, and lament, ye priests: howl, ye ministers of the altar: come, lie all night in sackcloth, ye ministers of my God: for the meat offering and the drink offering is withholden from the house of your God. Sanctify ye a fast, call a solemn assembly,

gather the elders and all the inhabitants of the land into the house of the Lord your God, and cry unto the Lord" (Joel 1:13-14).

"And there was one Anna, a prophetess, the daughter Phanuel, of the tribe of Aser: she was of a great age, and had lived with an husband seven years from her virginity: And she was a widow of about fourscore and four years, which departed not from the temple, but served God with fastings and prayers night and day" (Luke 2:36-37).

One of the most well known instances of coming aside to seek the Lord occurred when the Holy Spirit fell on the believers on the Day of Pentecost. They were all with one accord in one place in Jerusalem, as Jesus had instructed (Acts 2:1, Luke 24:49).

We see in Acts 1:14 that they had remained there "with one accord in prayer and supplication." For their obedience, God responded with miraculous power:

"And suddenly there came a sound from heaven as of a rushing mighty wind, and it filled all the house where they were sitting" (Acts 2:2).

Prayer and fasting are among our greatest weapons to fight the enemy. When we come aside and seek the Lord with our whole heart, soul and mind, we can expect supernatural results. This is a time of waiting on the Lord.

"But they that wait upon the Lord shall renew their strength; they shall mount up with wings as eagles; they shall run, and not be weary; and they shall walk, and not faint" (Isaiah 40:31).

"Wait on the Lord: be of good courage, and he shall strengthen thine heart: wait, I say, on the Lord" (Psalms 27:14).

Chapter 4

How to Seek the Lord

The word "seek" in 2 Chronicles 7:14 is the Hebrew word *baqash*, which means to search out or strive after, specifically in worship or prayer. It says,

> If my people, which are called by my name, shall *humble themselves*, and *pray*, and *seek my face*, and *turn from their wicked ways*; then will I *hear from heaven*, and will *forgive their sin*, and will *heal their land*."

In the shut-in we seek the Lord by praying for the manifestation of God's power. We strive for his deliverance and search for our needs to be met. We also worship him for the healing of our spirit, soul, and body.

The manifestation of his promises come from seeking the face of God through prayer and fasting as an act of obedience to the voice of God.

> "For he that cometh to God must believe that he is, and that he is a rewarder of them that diligently seek him" (Hebrew 11:6b).

Five Ways to Seek the Lord

Daniel proclaimed, "And I set my face unto the Lord God to seek by prayer and supplication with fasting and sackcloth and ashes" (Daniel 9:3). This indicates five ways to seek the Lord:

Prayer
Supplication
Fasting
Sackcloth
Ashes

Let's explore these further.

Prayer – Prayer is simply communicating with God. Jesus said, "Ask, and it shall be given you; seek, and ye shall find; knock, and it shall be opened unto you. For every one that asketh receiveth; and he that seeketh findeth; and to him that knocketh it shall be opened"(Matthew 7:7-8).

Dick Eastman, in his book *Change the World School of Prayer* (1983: A12-A15), provides some other very good definitions of prayer:

- Prayer is the first step to knowing Jesus Christ.
- Prayer is recognizing the presence of God.
- Prayer is man's means to know God intimately.
- Prayer is laying hold of God's promise.
- Prayer is the soul on its knees.
- Prayer is the path to strength and peace.
- Prayer is man's way to understand God's plan.
- Prayer is God's gift of power.
- Prayer is giving God access to our needs.
- Prayer is two people in love.

Eastman adds: "There is no circumstance or geographic location where prayer power is restricted. Prayer can penetrate places where no other power can reach. There is no situation or problem too great for the power of prayer. It leads to all blessings, taps all of God's power, and brings the prayer warriors into the very presence of God himself" (1983: A17).

Our Lord instructs believers to ask, seek, and knock. These three words cover the whole spectrum of praying:

We ask with the mind.
We seek with the soul.
We knock with the spirit.

In asking, we express a desire; in seeking we search for his direction; and in knocking, we show our determination. There are four ways we should pray:

1. Pray in faith. "And all things, whatsoever ye shall ask in prayer, believing, ye shall receive" (Matthew 21:22).
2. Pray with a pure heart. "If I regard iniquity in my heart the Lord will not hear me" (Psalms 66:18).
3. Pray with a forgiving spirit. "For if ye forgive men their trespasses, your heavenly Father will also forgive you" (Matthew 6:14).
4. Pray with expectation. "Therefore I say unto you, what things soever ye desire, when ye pray, believe that ye receive them, and ye shall have them" (Mark 11:24).

The intensity of our prayer life can be manifested in various ways. The scriptures highlight several outward demonstrations of an active prayer life. Some of the biblical demonstrations of such active prayer life include:

Supplication – This is a petition and urgent request of prayer (I Samuel 1:5-6, 10-13, 19-20). This is best illustrated by Hannah, a married woman, who had an urgent petition before God to conceive a son. The Lord answered her prayer.

"And it came to pass, as she continued praying before the LORD, that Eli marked her mouth. Now Hannah, she spake in her heart; only her lips moved, but her voice was not heard: therefore Eli thought she had been drunken. And Eli said unto her, How long wilt thou be drunken? put away thy wine from thee. And Hannah answered and said, No, my lord, I am a woman of a sorrowful spirit: I have drunk neither wine nor strong drink, but have poured out my soul before the LORD" (I Samuel 1:12-15).

Fasting – Fasting is self-denial for a spiritual reason. Biblical references to fasting refer to abstaining from food. Fasting conveyed a sacrifice of an individual's personal will, denoting the intensity of such spiritual needs and requests.

"Wherefore have we fasted, say they, and thou seest not? Wherefore have we afflicted our soul, and thou takest no knowledge? Behold, in the day of your fast ye find pleasure, and exact all your labours" (Isaiah 58:3).

Appendix C lists various biblical references to fasting and provide a good starting point to study the powerful results of this discipline.

Sackcloth – In biblical times death was so prevalent that rituals and symbols of mourning and grieving were established; sometimes in sophisticated and complex ways. The garment of sackcloth worn in biblical times was often an expression of internal struggles and emotions. It represented humility in the spirit of repentance and forgiveness. While we don't put on actual sackcloth today during a fast, we must maintain the same humility in our hearts if we desire supernatural results.

Ashes – Ashes are the powdery residue of burned material. In biblical times, to show mourning, the person would cover himself in ashes. This ancient practice developed into a deeper meaning of dying to self that God may be glorified. Self is the biggest enemy that we are fighting today. We must fight the good fight of faith, which is an internal struggle. This battle can be won through prayer and fasting.

These powerful biblical symbols are key components in conversing with God concerning situations in our lives, culture, community, nation and world. Once we apply these principles, we will see miraculous results. As Eastman says, quoting another writer, "The only limits to prayer are the limits of God. As far as God goes, prayer can go" (1983: A17).

Chapter 5

Fasting: Back to the Bible

G od's idea of an acceptable fast is described in detail in
Isaiah 58:

"Is not this the fast that I have chosen? to loose the
bands of wickedness, to undo the heavy burdens, and
to let the oppressed go free, and that ye break every
yoke?" (Isaiah 58:6).

Types of Fasts

There are various types of fasts. The following are over-
views of the three most frequent fasts, supported by biblical
references.

1. Absolute or Complete Fast

This fast involves total abstinence from food *and* water.

"And he caused it to be proclaimed and published
through Nineveh by the decree of the king and his
nobles, saying, "Let neither man nor beast, herd nor

flock, taste any thing: let them not feed, nor drink water" (Jonah 3:7).

"Go, gather together all the Jews that are present in Shushan, and fast ye for me, and neither eat nor drink three days, night or day: I also and my maidens will fast likewise; and so will I go in unto the king, which is not according to the law: and if I perish, I perish" (Esther 4:16).

"And he (Paul) was three days without sight, and neither did eat nor drink" (Acts 9:9).

2. Normal or Typical Fast

This fast is totally refraining from food and only drinking water. Distilled or bottled water is recommended. Drinking water flushes the toxins out of our bodies. Water is also the source of life and health. When Jesus fasted in the wilderness and with the multitude, it does not mention that they drank water or that they were thirsty. We can speculate, then, that they drank water and practiced a Normal or Typical Fast.

"Being 40 days tempted of the devil and in those days he did eat nothing: and when they were ended, he was afterwards hungry" (Luke 4:2).

"Then Jesus called his disciples unto him, and said, I have compassion on the multitude, because they continue with me now three days, and have nothing to eat: and I will not send them away fasting, lest they faint in the way" (Matthew 15:32).

During the shut-ins you can make your choice of an Absolute Fast or a Typical Fast. Keep in mind that some might feel weak from not eating, or they might have a headache from caffeine withdrawal, or stomach pains because they are hungry. We encourage you not to leave the shut-in for these reasons. Ask someone to pray for you and, if needed, drink a glass of juice.

3. Partial Fast (also known as the Daniel Fast)

This fast consists of vegetables only—no bread or other starches, no meat and no sweets. In addition, one who goes on a Daniel Fast must go for an extended period of time without food, including without vegetables. You are not making a sacrifice if you eat all day. We suggest hours such as from 12 a.m. to 12 p.m., or 12 a.m. to 3 p.m., or 12 a.m. to 6 p.m., or any other hours of your choice.

> "Prove thy servants, I beseech thee, ten days; and let them give us pulse to eat, and water to drink" (Daniel 1:12).

Who Can Fast?

According to the Bible, everyone can fast. When the disciples of John asked Jesus why his disciples did not fast, Jesus said that when he is taken from them, then they would fast (Matthew 9:15). In Matthew 6:16, Jesus cautioned his disciples "be not as the hypocrites."

> "Moreover when ye fast, be not as the hypocrites, of a sad countenance: for they disfigure their faces, that they may appear unto men to fast. Verily I say unto you, They have their reward."

Notice that he said, *when* and not *if* you fast. Jesus is therefore commanding believers—his disciples—to fast. If you've had difficulty fasting, you must remind yourself, "I can do all things through Christ which strengtheneth me" (Philippians 4:13). Fasting with others in a shut-in is an excellent opportunity to fast in a spiritual environment that can provide the support and encouragement you need to help you make it through your consecration.

Throughout the Old and New Testaments, fasting has been a lifestyle for God's people. Queen Esther proclaimed a fast before going to see the king to intercede for her people, the Jews.

> "Go, gather together all the Jews that are present in Shushan, and fast ye for me, and neither eat nor drink three days, night or day: I also and my maidens will fast likewise; and so will I go in unto the king, which is not according to the law: and if I perish, I perish."

Someone once asked me whether a woman who is expecting a baby or who is on her monthly cycle can or should fast. At first, I had no answer, but God brought Jonah 3:5-7 to my mind.

> "So the people of Nineveh believed God, and proclaimed a fast, and put on sackcloth, from the greatest of them even to the least of them. For word came unto the king of Nineveh, and he arose from his throne, and he laid his robe from him, and covered him with sackcloth, and sat in ashes. And he caused it to be proclaimed and published through Nineveh by the decree of the king and his nobles, saying, Let neither man nor beast, herd nor flock, taste any thing: let them not feed, nor drink water."

In Nineveh, it appears that the people fasted regardless of their condition. There were apparently no exemptions given. And this is only one case. The Lord never restricted anyone from participating in a call to fast—not with the fast called by Esther, or Jehoshaphat, or the king of Nineveh.

Nineveh was a large city. Chances are there were women who were pregnant or on their monthly cycle who were obedient to the call. Just as no one was exempted under the old covenant, Jesus' commandment to fast does not exempt anyone today. In this current day, many Christians do not seek God, but choose rather to put their faith solely in the doctors. Such was the habit of King Asa.

In 2 Chronicles 16:12, we read that he "...was diseased in his feet, until his disease was exceeding great: yet in his disease he sought not to the Lord, but to the physicians."

Asa succumbed under his condition simply because he refused to seek God. We thank God for the medical doctors and for their wonderful God-given contribution to improve the quality of our lives; however, all of our confidence and trust should not be in them when we have such unlimited access to our Great Physician.

I am for doctors, but I believe, "In all thy ways acknowledge him, and he shall direct thy paths" (Proverbs 3:6).

Chapter 6

Spiritual and Physical
of Benefits of Fasting

The powerlessness of modern day saints continues to be a problem in the world, just as it was for the disciples who walked with Jesus. They found themselves powerless to cast out a demon in a young boy. Then his father brought him to Jesus.

"And Jesus rebuked the devil; and he departed out of him: and the child was cured from that very hour. Then came the disciples to Jesus apart, and said, Why could not we cast him out? And Jesus said unto them, Because of your unbelief: for verily I say unto you, If ye have faith as a grain of mustard seed, ye shall say unto this mountain, Remove hence to yonder place; and it shall remove; and nothing shall be impossible unto you. Howbeit this kind goeth not out but by prayer and fasting" (Matthew 17:18-21).

When the disciples asked Jesus why they could not cast out the devil, Jesus said, "Because of your unbelief." However, he added, this kind of faith goes not out but by prayer and fasting. Through faith, Jesus said, we can cast out devils and lay hands on the sick and they shall recover (Mark 16:17-18). One of the greatest benefits of prayer and fasting is to destroy the spirit of unbelief.

Sadly, spiritual fasting is a dying discipline in most mainline churches and among professing Christians. However, there are spiritual and physical benefits in fasting. The spiritual benefits of fasting are summarized in Isaiah 58:6-8:

> "Is not this the fast that I have chosen? to loose the bands of wickedness, to undo the heavy burdens, and to let the oppressed go free, and that ye break every yoke? Is it not to deal thy bread to the hungry, and that thou bring the poor that are cast out to thy house? when thou seest the naked, that thou cover him; and that thou hide not thyself from thine own flesh? Then shall thy light break forth as the morning, and thine health shall spring forth speedily: and thy righteousness shall go before thee; the glory of the LORD shall be thy rereward" (Isaiah 58:6-8).

According to this scripture, fasting can bring the following spiritual benefits:

- To loose the bands of wickedness
- To undo the heavy burdens
- To let the oppressed go free
- That ye break every yoke
- To deal thy bread to the hungry
- That thou bring the poor that are cast out to thy house
- When thou seest the naked, that thou cover him
- That thou hid not thyself from thine own flesh
- Then shall they light break forth as the morning
- And thine health shall spring forth speedily

- And they righteousness shall go before thee
- The glory of the Lord shall be thy rereward

Other spiritual benefits include:

- Deliverance for the body of Christ
- Salvation and infilling of the Holy Ghost
- To witness the glory of God
- Faith to cast out devils
- Die to fleshly lust and carnality
- Victory over sin, shame and disgrace
- Mountain-top experience
- Ushering in the anointing
- Bringing forth revival
- Intensifying our prayer life
- Bringing our bodies under subjection
- A vacation with the Lord
- Freedom from oppression and depression
- Pulling down strongholds
- Spending prime time with the Lord
- Moving us from the natural to the supernatural

Physical Benefits of Fasting

Fasting is good for the entire body. It has been successful in treating all types of physical disorders. It restores health and lengthens our life span. Fasting makes it easy to overcome bad habits and addictions, such as tobacco, alcohol, etc. The physical benefits are many. Some that are most sought after are:

- Cleansing the body of toxins
- Restoring peace in the mind
- Healing homes and healing marriages
- Providing rest for the digestive system

- Destroying fear
- Bringing peace on our jobs

We have seen healings of cancer, diabetes, hypertension, headaches, asthma, and insomnia through the physical benefits of fasting.

Please see Appendix F for further reading on the physical benefits of fasting.

Chapter 7

Preparing Your Heart

M aking spiritual preparation is a critical step for the shut-in. We must prepare to seek the Lord. King Hezekiah prayed for the Israelites that the Lord would "... pardon every one that prepareth his heart to seek God..." (2 Chronicles 30:19). We are further reminded that King Rehoboam "...did evil, because he prepared not his heart to seek the Lord" (2 Chronicles 12:14).

Historically and biblically, those who did not prepare their hearts to seek the Lord did evil in his sight. So how do we cleanse our hearts? Repentance is the key. Repentance is a change of mind, a turning away from sin, disobedience, or rebellion, and turning to God. Repentance is the basis in seeking the face of the Lord. "If I regard iniquity in my heart, the Lord will not hear me" (Psalms 66:18).

We Must Repent

In order for God to hear our prayers, we must repent from our sins. Sin is the transgression of God's Law "Whosoever committeth sin transgresseth also the law: for sin is the transgression of the law" (I John 3:4). Sin enters our heart in three ways:

Sin can occur in thought. "For from within, out of the heart of men, proceed evil thoughts, adultery, fornications, murders, thefts, covetousness, wickedness, deceit, lasciviousness, an evil eye, blasphemy, pride, foolishness: All these evil things come from within, and defile the man" (Mark 7:21-23).

Sin can occur in word. "But I say unto you, That every idle word that men shall speak, they shall give account thereof in the day of judgment. For by thy words thou shalt be justified, and by thy words that thou shalt be condemned" (Matthew 12:36-37).

Sin can occur in deeds. "Mortify therefore your members which are upon the earth; fornication, uncleanness, inordinate affection, evil concupiscence, and covetousness, which is idolatry: For which things' sake the wrath of God cometh on the children of disobedience: In the which ye also walked some time, when ye lived in them. But now ye also put off all these; anger, wrath, malice, blasphemy, filthy communication out of your mouth. Lie not one to another, seeing that ye have put off the old man with his deeds" (Col. 3:5-9).

There are sins of omission and sins of commission. We commit the sins of omission when we neglect to do what the law of God requires. Examples include:

- *Unholy living and lifestyles* – "But as he which hath called you is holy, so be ye holy in all manner of conversation; Because it is written, 'Be ye holy; for I am holy'" (1 Peter 1:15-16).
- *Lack of prayer life* – "And he spake a parable unto them to this end, that men ought always to pray, and not to faint" (Luke 18:1).
- *Refraining from fasting* – "Therefore also now, says the Lord, turn ye even to me with all your heart, and with fasting, and with weeping, and with moaning" (Joel 2:12).

- ***Refusal to witness and disciple others*** – The Holy Ghost can help us be a more effective witness. "But ye shall receive power, after that the Holy Ghost is come upon you: and ye shall be witnesses unto me both in Jerusalem, and in all Judaea, and in Samaria, and unto the uttermost part of the earth" (Acts 1:8).
- ***Slothfulness in church attendance*** – "Not forsaking the assembling of ourselves together, as the manner of some is; but exhorting one another: and so much the more, as ye see the day approaching" (Hebrews 10:25).
- ***Not being charitable*** – "Every man according as he purposeth in his heart, so let him give; not grudgingly, or of necessity: for God loveth a cheerful giver" (2 Corinthians 9:7).
- ***Disobedience*** – "Behold, to obey is better than sacrifice, and to hearken than the fat of rams" (I Samuel 15:22b).
- ***Unfaithfulness*** – "Be thou faithful unto death, and I will give thee a crown of life" (Revelation 2:10b).

The sin of commission is when we do what the law of God forbids. These works of the flesh are highlighted in Galatians 5:19-21:

- ***Adultery*** – A married person having sex outside of marriage. (Exodus 20:14)
- ***Fornication*** – Having sex without being married. "But fornication, and all uncleanness, or covetousness, let it not be once named among you, as becometh saints" (Ephesians 5:3). And, "For this is the will of God, even your sanctification that ye should abstain from fornication" (I Thessalonians 4:3).
- ***Uncleanness*** – Not pure morally, evil, dirty, filthy; i.e., oral sex. Some people say that it is okay to

commit oral sex because it is not really sex. Oral sex may not be sex, but it is sin. I have heard that what you do in your bedroom is okay, but sin is sin wherever it is committed. (I Thessalonians 4:1-8)

- *Lasciviousness* – Feeling or exhibiting lust. (Proverbs 6:25-26, Matthew 5:28)
- *Idolatry* – The worship of something created as opposed to the worship of the Creator. (Isaiah 40:19, Exodus 20:4-6, Ephesians 5:5)
- *Witchcraft* – Magic, sorcery, divination, occult practices such as fortune-telling, astrology, channeling, voodoo. (Deuteronomy 18:10-12)
- *Hatred* – Strong dislike toward someone or something. (Titus 3:3)
- *Variance* – Hostile confrontation, discord, quarrel, belligerence. (Colossians 3:13)
- *Emulations* – To rival with someone for success; to compete against. (Romans 11:14)
- *Wrath/violence* – Anger displayed in action and rage. (James 1:19-20)
- *Strife* – Quarreling, conflict and contention. (Proverbs 17:1)
- *Seditions* – Conduct or language inviting rebellion against the authority or a state or lawful government. (Galatians 5:20)
- *Heresies* – False doctrine or teaching that denies one of the fundamental beliefs of the church, such as the Lordship or Deity of Jesus Christ. (2 Peter 2:1-3)
- *Envying/greed* – A feeling or resentment of jealousy toward others because of their possessions or character. (James 3:14-16); Selfish ambition. (Romans 13:13, I Peter 2:1)
- *Homicide* – Unlawful killing of one person by another, especially with premeditated malice. (Genesis 4:8-10)

- *Drunkenness/addictions* – Result from drinking intoxicating beverages and/or addictions to illegal drugs, gambling, gluttony, overindulgences. (Proverbs 20:1)
- *Revellings* – Wild/disorderly parties, rebellion. (1 Peter 4:3)
- *Filthy conversation* – Gossip, cursing, pornography. (2 Peter 2:7)
- *Vile affections* – Homosexuality/Lesbianism: "For this cause God gave them up unto vile affections: for even their women did change the natural use into that which is against nature: And likewise also the men, leaving the natural use of the woman, burned in their lust one toward another; men with men working that which is unseemly, and receiving in themselves that recompense of their error which was meet" (Romans 1:26-27). And, "Thou shalt not lie with mankind, as with womankind: it is abomination" (Leviticus 18:22).

Needless to say, sins of omission and commission contribute to a broken relationship with Christ, others and yourself. No spiritual breakthrough can occur unless there is a genuine acknowledgement of our brokenness and shame. Do not miss a divine opportunity during a Sixty-Hour Consecration without this major step: repentance.

"If we confess our sins, he is faithful and just to forgive us our sins, and to cleanse us from all unrighteousness" (I John 1:9).

Ask the people to bow their heads and to repent of their sins. Express that we must:

Repent,

Believe, and

Receive God's forgiveness from our sins.

Now we are ready to step into Romans 12:1, which states:

"I beseech you therefore, brethren, by the mercies of God, that ye present your bodies a living sacrifice, holy, acceptable unto God, which is your reasonable service."

Whatever condition or situation you are in, you can be totally delivered through prayer and fasting. You can live a victorious life through Jesus Christ.

The Purpose of Fasting

One must have a *purpose* for fasting. Throughout the Bible, the people fasted out of obedience to God and leadership and for a specific purpose.

- Esther and the Jews fasted for God to save them from extermination.
- The king and the people of Nineveh fasted for God to spare their city from destruction. (Jonah 3:5-7)
- Jehoshaphat fasted for victory over three invading armies—spiritual intervention. (2 Chronicles 20:3-4)
- Jesus fasted because he was led by the Spirit. (Luke 4:1-2)
- Samuel led the people to repentance through fasting. (I Samuel 7:3-6)
- Israel fasted confessing the sins and iniquities of their fathers. (Nehemiah 9:1-2)

- Ezra fasted for guidance and a safe journey and protection from their enemies. (Ezra 8:23)
- Paul (Saul) and Barnabas fasted for preparation and direction. Acts 13:2)
- Paul fasted for the right leadership. (Acts 14:23)
- Anna had a lifestyle of prayer and fasting. (Luke 2:36-38)

Chapter 8

Shut-In Preparations: Churches and Individuals

The organization that hosts a shut-in must be diligent to prepare for the consecration to ensure that the participants maximize their experience. There are also preparations that the individual must make. Preparations for individuals and organizations are listed in this chapter.

Remember, the more informed a person is the better the outcome will be. The benefits will be a spiritual experience that will affect the lives of the people in a profound and supernatural way. Preparation also helps bring oneness, in addition a new level of joy, gladness, love and truth through the regular practice of prayer and fasting. Zechariah 8:18-23 states:

> "And the word of the Lord of hosts came unto me, saying, Thus saith the Lord of hosts; The fast of the fourth month, and the fast of the fifth, and the fast of the seventh, and the fast of the tenth, shall be to the house of Judah joy and gladness, and cheerful feasts; therefore love the truth and peace. Thus said the Lord of hosts; it shall yet come to pass, that there

shall come people and the inhabitants of many cities: And the inhabitants of one city shall go to another saying, Let us go speedily to pray before the Lord, and to seek the Lord of hosts: I will go also.

"Yea, many people and strong nations shall come to seek the Lord of hosts in Jerusalem, and to pray before the Lord. Thus saith the Lord of hosts; In those days it shall come to pass, that ten men shall take hold out of all languages of the nations, even shall take hold of the skirt of him that is a Jew, saying, We will go with you: for we have heard that God is with you."

The entire body of Christ will experience a spiritual revolution if we hear and obey in this matter of fasting and praying. The shut-in ministry is to bless and strengthen the local church or conference where the shut-in revival is conducted. The long-term results of spiritual maturity and growth are the genuine success of any shut-in. The short-term result is that churches will be able to restore this art of spiritual awakening so vital to any generation.

The following are some basic recommendations to help ensure a smooth and successful Sixty-Hour Consecration:

Individual Preparation

Preparation for the Sixty-Hour Consecration must begin well in advance of the actual date of the shut-in. Individuals should determine their specific purpose for the fast, and have a general idea of what fasting entails. I suggest that you write down your purpose to help stay focused on what you are seeking from the Lord. Know that this is a discipline and a sacrifice that God honors and rewards.

Physical Preparation

It is advisable to modify your eating habits and caffeine intake a few days before the fast. This will rid your body of some of the toxins that may cause headaches, stomachaches, or other physical challenges during the fast.

When preparing for a shut-in it is important to do things decently and in order. Wives and husbands should have permission from their spouses to fast and to be away from home for the designated time. This will enable the other party to be informed and to respect the fast.

Those who have small children should either make sure that they are in competent hands or bring them to the shut-in. While it may not be the most convenient arrangement, there is a biblical precedent for children fasting. In 2 Chronicles 20, we learn that when King Jehoshaphat called a fast to seek God's protection from the invading armies, everyone fasted.

"And Jehoshaphat feared, and set himself to seek the Lord, and proclaimed a fast throughout all Judah (verse 3); ...and all Judah stood before the Lord, with their little ones, their wives, and their children" (verse 13).

Practical Preparation

I offer the following practical suggestions for getting ready for this spiritual time:

- Plan to block the shut-in dates on your calendar. Refrain from scheduling any appointments during the three-day experience.
- If you will be traveling from a distance to get to the shut-in, factor in traveling time before and after the

shut-in revival so that you do not schedule appointments or events too close to the departure and travel
times.

• Invite family and friends to join you in all or a portion
of the revival. Inform them that although they are
welcome to attend with you, the shut-in is deeply
personal and not a social event. You must resist being
distracted from seeking the face of the Lord. If there
is someone that you feel should know of your where-
abouts, be sure to give them the church address and
phone number of the shut-in location where you can
be reached in case of an emergency.

• Fully charge your cell phone before arriving as there
may only be a limited number of electrical outlets
available onsite to recharge your phone.

• Since the actual shut-in portion of the consecration
spans Thursday night through Saturday noon, plan to
limit your calls only to emergencies.

• If you are under medical supervision, inform your
doctor of your plans. If given approval to attend,
make certain you follow all medical requirements as
it pertains to prescription medicines.

• If you are on any dietary restrictions and/or may need
to eat food for medical reasons, ensure that you follow
dietary requirements as prescribed by your physician.
Notwithstanding, it is your personal faith decision to
choose not to comply with your doctor's orders. The
host organization cannot be held responsible for your
choice. We have many documented testimonies of
people who acted in faith and refused their medications. Again, this is a personal decision. Since this is a
healing ministry of deliverance (physically, emotionally, and spiritually), some with a terminal prognosis may desire to act in faith. After all, you will

be spending time with the Great Physician; human extremity is divine opportunity.

What to Bring to the Church

Every effort must be made to respect and protect the local church property. During the break periods where there is opportunity for respite and sleep, ensure something is placed under your head and body to protect the pews from being soiled by saliva, hair oils/gels, ink pens, or other items. You should also refrain from putting your shoes on the pews.

We also urge you to leave expensive valuables at home or prepare to lock your luggage. Neither the local church nor the shut-in ministry is responsible for lost or stolen items.

The following is a checklist of suggested items to bring to the shut-in. The items are not required but are recommendations only. Feel free to choose among these or to bring other items that fit your interests and purposes.

- Bible
- Pen/pencil and paper
- Devotional booklets for personal quiet time reading
- Personal bottle of olive oil (labeled with your name) to be blessed
- Handkerchiefs or other pieces of cloth to be blessed
- Bottled water (may be provided by host church)
- Toiletries and personal items (towel/washcloth)
- Hand sanitizers/towel wipes
- Kleenex
- Mouthwash/liquid drops/breath spray
- Toothbrush/toothpaste
- Comfortable, appropriate clothing and shoes
- Change of clothing

- Sleeping bag, air mattress (if space permits) or flat sheets and a blanket to sleep on the church pew or chairs
- Pillow
- Scarf or towel to put under your head

Host Organization Preparation

The shut-in ministry is an asset to the body of Christ and, in particular, an extension to the ministry of the local church. In my experience over the many years of conducting such powerful revivals, many churches were unfamiliar with this critical Christian art form and how to prepare their local congregations for such a powerful spiritual opportunity.

Since many old traditional and cultural misunderstandings of a shut-in are prevalent, it is important to instruct local churches, Christian conferences, conventions, convocations, and interfaith fellowships how to prepare for a shut-in revival. Every effort should be made to focus on allowing the spiritual breakthrough needed during the Sixty-Hour Consecration. Such revivals must be orchestrated by the Holy Spirit through prayerful individuals with the intention of equipping and building believers to higher levels of personal and spiritual maturity.

The following are some practical tips for planning and organizing the shut-in:

- Plan in advance.
- Establish dates, giving ample time for proper preparation.
- Ensure that the Sixty-Hour Consecration is adequately announced in all services, church bulletins, Web sites, television, and/or radio announcements.

- Keep the shut-in ministry leader who is conducting the revival informed of any changes, additions, deletions or other matters affecting the actual event.
- Ensure that there are no conflicts of interest or scheduling conflicts that will hamper the services.
- Encourage all church officials and members to participate in the full Sixty-Hour Consecration, if possible.
- Notify all persons participating in the revival to prepare prayerfully for the shut-in. This includes scripture readers, soloists, choirs, and designated speakers.
- Prepare to distribute copies of *Teaching on the Anointing* (See chapter 9, page 75).

Safety and Security Issues

Identify all security issues to ensure that the church facility, including parking, is properly secured. Designate adequate and secure parking for those who are remaining for the entire shut-in. Ensure that proper fire extinguishers, smoke detectors, and exit doors are in working order, and that they are marked and identified for emergency purposes.

Chapter 9

Shut-In Schedule:
The Sixty-Hour Consecration

Although the shut-in ministry team has developed a working agenda for the Sixty-Hour Consecration, the schedule is directed by the Holy Spirit rather than by set times. Therefore, participants are strongly encouraged to avoid being overly concerned about the time or the next item on the agenda. The trained shut-in ministry team will be able to facilitate the process while flowing with the movement of the Holy Spirit over the three-day gathering.

During the shut-in, we endeavor to minister to the whole person: spirit, soul, and body.

We minister to the spirit by being filled or refilled by the Holy Spirit. To minister to the soul, we are fed by the word of God. To minister to the body, it is important that we rest during break times so we can all be in prayer together. The entire experience is for the spiritual renewal of God's people. Such renewal is a result of ministering to the whole person.

The Sixty-Hour Consecration covers the time span from Wednesday midnight to Saturday noon. Throughout the shut-in, the prayer hours are 9, 12, 3 and 6 around the clock (with the exception of Friday night, when the prayer begins at 7 p.m. due to the One-Night Revival; and on Saturday, when there is no 9 a.m. prayer due to the Jericho March and other activities).

The foundation for the one-hour of prayer is in Matthew 26:40 where Jesus asked his disciples to watch with him for one hour while he prayed.

In this chapter, we will look at the shut-in schedule, the various activities involved in the shut-in experience, and the scriptural basis for each. The schedule and activities presented are recommendations only and can be changed as the shut-in ministry team feels led of the Lord.

WEDNESDAY

12 midnight   The fast begins in the participant's home. The next 60 hours will test their commitment and their faith. They will learn that the flesh never wants to make such a sacrifice. Of course, the temptations and distractions will be fewer once they enter into the house of God on Thursday evening and find strength in uniting with others seeking the face of God.

THURSDAY

8 p.m.   Participants enter the house of God. They come with a spirit of expectancy.

9 p.m.   **One-Hour Prayer:** The first prayer of the shut-in continues for one hour. All participants are asked to get into their preferred prayer position. The scriptures document several prayer postures:

Kneeling: "He went into his house; and his windows being open in his chamber toward Jerusalem, he kneeled upon his knees three times a day, and prayed, and gave thanks before his God, as he did aforetime" (Daniel 6:10).

Sitting: "And David the king came and sat before the Lord" (1 Chronicles 17:16).

Standing: "And he stood before the altar of the Lord in the presence of all the congregation of Israel, and spread forth his hands" (2 Chronicles 6:12).

Bowing: "O come, let us worship and bow down: let us kneel before the LORD our maker" (Psalms 95:6).

Prostrate: "And Abram fell on his face: and God talked with him" (Genesis 17:3).

10 p.m. **Songs of Praise:** "...come before his presence with singing" (Psalms 100:2). Singing can cleanse us of negative emotions and usher us into the presence of God. After the first hour of prayer, the group will sing a song of praise. The specific songs selected is at the discretion of the leader.

Welcoming of Participants: The host pastor or his designee welcomes the congregation and informs them of the church facilities that will be utilized during the shut-in. All guests

71

who are not members of the host church are asked to stand and give their name, pastor's name, church affiliation and city. You may modify this procedure in cases of larger meetings such as conferences or convocations. The shut-in leader shares the word of God on praying and fasting.

Scripture Reading and Teaching: This section will provide instruction on how to seek the Lord. We will use scripture, responsive reading, definitions and discussion to gain a clear understanding of this primary purpose of our shut-in.

Scripture Reading: 2 Chronicles 20:1-30 – The leader reminds everyone to stop at every period, pause at the commas and to take time to comprehend the scripture. We read responsively, i.e., the leader reads the first verse and the congregation reads the next verse and so on, with the last verse read in unison by the leader and congregation. We next discuss the topic of how to seek the Lord.

Teaching: How to seek the Lord (See chapters 3 and 4)

12 midnight   **Prayer of Agreement:** "Jesus said, 'Again I say unto you, that if two of you shall agree on earth concerning anything that they shall ask, it shall be done for them by My Father who is in Heaven. For where two or three are

gathered together in My name, there am I in the midst of them'" (Matthew 18:19-20).

We are a "Body" ministry, which means that the body of Christ is more than an organization—it is a living organism. Our coming together in the name of the Lord Jesus Christ binds us in agreement to each other.

"How should one chase a thousand, and two put ten thousand to flight" (Deuteronomy 32:30).

"Now unto him that is able to do exceeding abundantly above all that we ask or think, according to the power that worketh in us" (Ephesians 4:20).

What a powerful force when we unite our forces together in prayer and fasting. Participants stand one at a time and give their individual prayer requests. The shut-in leader or designee will ask someone to stand and pray for that participant who expressed a certain need. If others in the congregation have the same type of need, those persons are asked to come forth. Prayer is offered for the entire group expressing such needs. The congregation comes in agreement with the person or persons who gives such a request. The Prayer of Agreement continues until 1 a.m.

FRIDAY

1 a.m.   **Break:** During this break (or quiet time) the congregants may sleep, read or pray quietly. We encourage those in attendance to make use of this and all other break times to rest as a vital means of spiritual recuperation. Although this rest period may be contrary to some beliefs, this is what God has given me for his people.

3 a.m.   **Congregational Prayer:** Any person desiring to lead prayer is given an opportunity to do so within this hour.
                Scripture Reading: Isaiah 58 (God's chosen fast)

4 a.m.   **Break:** (Sleeping, Resting, Reading, Quiet Time, Silence)

6 a.m.   **Paul and Silas Prayer:** This time will consist of praying and singing. One person will lead a song and another person will pray about that song or vice versa. This will continue for one hour.

> "And at midnight Paul and Silas prayed, and sang praises unto God: and the prisoners heard them. And suddenly there was a great earthquake, so that the foundations of the prison were shaken: and immediately all the doors were opened, and every one's bands were loosed" (Acts 16:25-26).

7 a.m.   **Scripture   Reading:** Joel   2   is   read
responsively.

Teaching on the Anointing: The anointing
demonstrates the presence and the power of
God (Isaiah 10:27). And it shall come to pass
in that day, that his burden shall be taken
away from off thy shoulder and his yoke from
off thy neck, and the yoke shall be destroyed
because of the anointing. The Hebrew word
for anointing is *mashach*," to rub or smear
with oil; to consecrate; to paint."
    Each time the term is read from the Old
Testament pertaining to one who is anointed
of God, it is pronounced *mashiyak*.
    Anointing in the Old Testament demon-
strated activities of God's priests and prophets
of a spiritual reality. This reality in the New
Testament is Jesus Christ, the Anointed One,
sent by God to reconcile the world to God.
When oil was used to anoint, it represented
this deep biblical spiritual meaning of recon-
ciliation. We experience the presence and
power of God in consecration by receiving
this anointing, reconciling ourselves to
Christ.
    Our time of consecration is for us to
symbolically hold on to the horn of the altar.
"But my horn shalt thou exalt like the horn of
a unicorn: I shall be anointed with fresh oil"
(Psalms 92:10).
    A horn is a symbol of strength. A unicorn
or wild ox symbolizes awesome power. This
symbolism of strength demonstrates the
power of God in our lives. This is evident by

75

the means of praying and fasting. As a wild ox commands its own space, the anointing of God in our lives commands Satan to be put under our feet.

This spiritual warfare cannot be achieved by human means, but through the power of God's Spirit and word. "Not by might, nor power but by my Spirit, saith the Lord" (Zechariah 4:6). We observe the process of this anointing through the proclamation of the Word.

> "The Spirit of the Lord is upon me, because he hath anointed me to preach the gospel to the poor; he hath sent me to heal the brokenhearted, to preach deliverance to the captives, and recovering of sight to the blind, to set at liberty them that are bruised, to preach the acceptable year of the Lord" (Luke 4:18-19).

The Spirit of the Lord comes in us when we accept him as our Lord and Savior Jesus Christ. The Spirit of the Lord comes upon us to do ministry.

Jesus the Messiah, the Christ, the Lord, the Anointed One declared his purpose: Preaching to the poor, healing those who are discouraged, preaching deliverance to those in captivity, recovery to those who are blinded, setting free the wounded and preaching the day of the Lord (Luke 4:18-19). Jesus as our model announced that the purpose of his anointing was to minister to the whole person—body, mind and spirit.

Additional scriptures to stress this understanding of the anointing for consecration include the following:

"And it shall come to pass in that day, that his burden shall be taken away from off thy shoulder, and his yoke from off thy neck, and the yoke shall be destroyed because of the anointing" (Isaiah 10:27).

"How God anointed Jesus of Nazareth with the Holy Ghost and with power: who went about doing good, and healing all that were oppressed of the devil; for God was with him" (Acts 10:38).

"Now he which stablisheth us with you in Christ, and hath anointed us, is God" (2 Corinthians 1:21).

"Cast me not away from thy presence; and take not thy Holy Spirit from me. We say like David, Lord if you take everything from us, do not take your Holy Spirit" (Psalms 51:11).

"Thou hast loved righteousness and hated iniquity; therefore God, even thy God, hath anointed thee with the oil of gladness above thy fellows" (Hebrew 1:9).

"And it came to pass, as they were burying a man that, behold, they spied a band of men; and they cast the man into the sepulcher of Elisha: and when the man was let down, and touched the bones of Elisha, he revived, and stood up on his feet" (2 Kings 13:21).

Elisha was so anointed that the dead man touched his bones and was revived. We should long for that type of anointing.

"Insomuch that they brought forth the sick into the streets, and laid them on beds and couches, that at the least the shadow of Peter passing by might overshadow some of them" (Acts 5:15).

Peter's anointing was so great that his shadow brought healing and deliverance.

"Moreover when ye fast, be not, as the hypocrites, of a sad countenance: for they disfigure their faces, that they may appear unto men to fast. Verily I say unto you, they have their reward. But thou, when thou fastest, anoint thine head, and wash thy face" (Matthew 6:16-17).

After the teaching about the anointing, the leader will instruct on the significance of the anointing oil and the purpose of the Anointing Service.

Information on the Anointing Oil: The anointing oil is to anoint our heads and not our clothes. Far too many people anoint their hands and then put their hands on the clothing of others, diminishing the purpose of the act of anointing. Oil is difficult to remove from clothing. This event is not to bathe in oil and soil clothing, but to proceed into the deeper meaning of consecration.

"Thou preparest a table before me in the presence of mine enemies: thou anointest my head with oil: my cup runneth over" (Psalm 23:5).

Anointing Service: At this time, everyone is asked to enter into the center aisle in the sanctuary or facility where the shut-in is being held and to stand two by two. The leader will distribute two bottles of oil to be passed. In the case of a larger attendance, several bottles of oil will be passed.

The leader will ask those present to place oil on their right index finger. Everyone will wait until all have placed oil on their right index finger. When all receive the oil and place it on their right index finger, each person will anoint their own foreheads.

Afterwards, they will face the person beside them and tell the other person why they want to be anointed. It could be for a ministry, or for some other purpose. Each believer will lift their partner's request up in prayer. After both have finished praying, they will return to their seats for further instruction by the shut-in leader. "Anointing Fall on Me" or some other suitable song can be sung at the time of the passing of the oil.

Preparation for the Day's Sessions: The shut-in leader or his/her designee will ask for three volunteers to read scripture and three volunteers to minister at the following times: 9 a.m., 12 p.m., and 3 p.m. This unrehearsed approach is to continue to allow the Holy Spirit to operate in the consecration. Scriptures may be selected based upon what has been given to the individual to share with participants. Sermons should be no longer than fifteen minutes and should bring edification and encouragement to those who are present. This period will end with a break prior to the Prayer Walk.

9 a.m.

Prayer Walk

"Every place that the sole of your foot shall tread upon, that have I given unto you, as I said unto Moses" (Joshua 1:3).

The Prayer Walk consists of groups of two or three-person teams from the congregation going out into the neighborhood of the church, praying, witnessing, evangelizing and distributing tracts with the church's address and phone number.

The most important purpose for the Prayer Walk is to invite people to accept Christ into their lives. You can also invite them to the shut-in and to the church's regular services. Volunteers walk throughout the neighborhood, stopping and praying at each house in a one-block radius. The teams pray against drug houses, prostitution, gangs, liquor stores, etc.

Those remaining in the church will participate by taking turns praying. Individuals will be praying for needs in the North, South, East, and West. The shut-in leader or designee will state to the congregation what they will need to pray about in each direction of the sanctuary. Some examples are *schools, residential areas, hospitals, fire stations, police stations, liquor stores, strip clubs, drug houses, poverty, prostitution, gang activities, drug smuggling, internet pornography, runaway children, church dissension, halfway houses, alcohol rehabilitation centers, abortion clinics, local jails, senior citizen centers, mental health institutions, foster care homes, colleges, universities, grocery stores, shopping centers, airports, bus and train stations, power plants, local businesses, corrupt businesses, financial institutions, the homeless, abused children, social security office, the unemployment office, health and human services offices, recreational centers, libraries, burglars, murderers, unwed mothers, teen pregnancies, rapists, kidnappers, sexual predators and offenders.*

Judy Garlow Wade has written an excellent book on how to have a Prayer Walk. It is entitled *Take the Name of Jesus with You.* You may find it helpful in planning and executing a Prayer Walk. When the groups return from the Prayer Walk, one of the team members from each group will give highlights of their experience. Often some of the people whom they witnessed to will come to the service.

10 a.m. **Scripture Reading and the Word of God (short message):** Concludes with a break until 12 p.m.

11 a.m. **Break:** (Sleeping, Resting, Reading, Quiet Time, Silence)

12 p.m. **Teaching on Prayer of Confession:** James reminds us, "Confess your faults one to another, and pray one for another, that ye may be healed" (James 5:16). You prepare your heart to receive from the Lord by following these three steps:

1. Ask God to forgive you for your past mistakes, shortcomings and, weaknesses. "If I regard iniquity in my heart, the Lord will not hear me" (Psalms 66:18).
2. Ask God to forgive the persons who hurt you, abused you or misused you. "Then said Jesus, Father, forgive them for they know not what they do" (Luke 23:34a).
3 Ask God to forgive you for holding unforgiveness in your heart. "If we confess our sins, he is faithful and just to forgive us our sins, and to cleanse us from all unrighteousness" (I John 1:9).

You would be wise to remind yourself of the following:

To forgive yourself; let go of the
condemnation.
Forgive others so that unforgiveness will not
block your relationship with God.
To remember that forgiveness is emotionally
rewarding.
Unforgiveness will destroy you through sick-
ness and even death.
Forgiveness cleans our hearts and brings
answers to prayer.

Prayer of Confession: It's time to practice
making your confession. Everyone is asked to
pair off in groups of two. The leader will give
the instruction for each person to share and
confess their faults to a partner in their group.
It is recommended that you select someone
you may feel comfortable in sharing with.

After you have selected a partner, you may
go to a private place in the church. The location within the church is not important. What
is most significant is sharing with someone
areas of personal harmful secrets and guilt
that keeps you from spiritual maturity. This
session often lasts from twenty to thirty
minutes. Prayer for healing from harmful
secrets and guilt are to be offered. What is
shared in secret should be kept in secret.

Afterwards, circles of six should be
formed. All within that group are asked to
share how God blessed them in their group of
two. After all have shared within the group,
one person will pray, closing the session.
Each person will return to his or her seat to
hear the reading of the Word.

1 p.m.	**Scripture Reading and the Word of God (short message):** Concludes with a break time until 3 p.m.
1:30 p.m.	**Break:** (Sleeping, Resting, Reading, Quiet Time, Silence)
3 p.m.	**Prayer for those in Authority:** In I Timothy 2:1-4, Paul admonishes us to pray for those in authority. "I exhort therefore, that, first of all, supplications, prayers, intercessions, and giving of thanks, be made for all men; For kings, and for all that are in authority; that we may lead a quiet and peaceable life in all godliness and honesty. For this is good and acceptable in the sight of God our Saviour. Who will have all men to be saved, and to come unto the knowledge of the truth."

At this one-hour prayer, the leader selects or various individuals volunteer to pray for those in authority in the general categories set forth below. Appendix B lists additional details of individuals and groups to intercede for within each of these categories.

Government Leaders
Spiritual Leaders
Armed Forces
Justice System
Peace and Safety Officers
Educational System
Medical Professionals
Family Authorities
Financial and Other Institutions

4 p.m.   **Scripture Reading and the Word of God
           (short message):** At this time, the leader
           will solicit four volunteers to lead 15-
           minute prayer segments at the 7 p.m. prayer.
           Concludes with a break time until 6:45 p.m.
           (Everyone is asked to move all personal
           belongings to a designated area in the church
           for the sanctuary to be free of clutter for the
           night service.)

4:30 p.m. **Break:** (Sleeping, Resting, Reading, Quiet
           Time, Silence)

7 p.m.   **One-Hour Prayer (start of the One-Night
           Revival)**

8 p.m.   **Scripture Reading:** "Search the scriptures;
           for in them ye think ye have eternal life:
           and they are they which testify of me" (John
           5:39).

           Scripture Search: Preaching, praising, and
           praying are important elements in a Sixty-
           Hour Consecration. However, we must search
           and be taught from the scriptures. Teaching
           was always a primary component of our
           Lord's ministry. In fact, Nicodemus referred
           to Jesus as Rabbi (which means teacher)
           (John 3:2). Throughout the gospels, we read
           about Jesus teaching his disciples.
               In our time of Scripture Search, we are
           reminded of the value of teaching scriptural
           truth in our consecration. The shut-in leader
           or whoever is designated will ask volun-

teers from the congregation to find a single scripture in the Bible which represents a command, a promise, or a significant Bible fact. Volunteers will stand and read the scripture and state its location in the Bible. The leader will offer two clarifying examples, one from the Old Testament and one from the New Testament. Some Old Testament examples are:

> *Command:* "Thou shall not steal" (Exodus 20:15).
>
> *Promise:* "The Lord shall cause thine enemies that rise up against thee to be smitten before thy face: they shall come out against thee one way, and flee before thee seven ways" (Deut. 28:7).
>
> *Fact:* "In the beginning God created the heaven and the earth" (Genesis 1:1).

Some scriptures, such as 2 Chronicles 20:17, encompass all three:

> "Ye shall not need to fight in this battle, set yourselves, stand ye still, and see the salvation of the Lord with you, O Judah and Jerusalem: fear not, nor be dismayed; tomorrow go out against them: for the Lord will be with you."

The leader will also give an example of qualifying scriptures from the New Testament:

Command: "Put on therefore, as the elect of God, holy and beloved, bowels of mercies, kindness, humbleness of mind, meekness, longsuffering" (Col. 3:12).

Fact: "In the beginning was the Word, and the Word was with God, and the Word was God" (John 1:1).

Promise: "And, behold, I come quickly; and my reward is with me, to give every man according as his work shall be" (Revelation 22:12).

Those who are participating in this challenge, simply stand and state whether the scripture that is about to be read is a command, fact, promise, or all three. No other comments are necessary. This is not a game but a method of getting the word into the hearts of the people.

Praise and Worship: This is the time that we all come together to praise and magnify God in the beauty of holiness. We come to exalt God in song. A praise and worship team will minister in song for approximately ten-fifteen minutes.

Overcoming Testimonies: Three or four congregants will give their testimonies relating to the shut-in, either past or present. This is a time of sharing with others what God has done to build their faith. It is inspiring and also builds the faith of the hearers. "And they overcame him by the blood of the Lamb, and by the words of their testimony" (Revelation 12:11a).

Congregational Song: "Come before his presence with singing" (Psalms 100:2). Singing can cleanse us of negative emotions and usher us into the presence of God.

9 p.m.

Circle Prayer: The shut-in leader or designee will say: Let us prepare out hearts to receive from the Lord by asking for forgiveness according to Psalms 66:18 which reads: "If I regard iniquity in my heart, the Lord will not hear me."

As there will be many attending the shut-in for the One-Night Revival and may have not had the opportunity to participate in the act of repentance and forgiveness, all are asked to stand and to get into groups of five or six. At this time, everyone is asked to bow their heads and to repent and ask God for forgiveness. The leader, under the inspiration of the Holy Ghost will give the topic of the prayer. Each person is asked to give a prayer request based on the prayer focus. An example of a prayer focus is "peace."

Within the groups of five or six, one individual may ask for peace in their home; another peace in their family; another peace in their church; another peace in their life; and another peace with God. After each person has shared their request, one person in each group is asked to pray a closing prayer.

The leader is not limited to an exclusive topic for this activity. Based on the guidance of the Holy Spirit other topics may be used. Such as *salvation, hindrance, discourage-ment, joy, self-control, meekness, humility, love, faithfulness, loving-kindness, tempta-tion, suffering, despair, uncleanness, hatred, wrath, heresies, envyings, gentleness, good-ness, faith, meekness, forgiveness, fellowship, charity.* When the prayers are concluded, participants are instructed to return to their seats.

Musical Selection (by choir, singing group, or soloist)

Prayer for Pastors and Churches: One person from each church represented by those present will come forward and form a line in front of the congregation. Each one is asked to give his name, the name of their church, the pastor's name, city and state. The pastor of the host church or designated individual will pray and ask God's blessings on each church or fellowship that is represented.

Freewill Offering: To help cover the expenses of the revival

Musical Selection (by choir, singing group, or soloist)

Message from the Word of God: Your choice of speaker

Deliverance Service: The ministry of deliv-erance is conducted by the shut-in leader or the speaker of the hour. It is a response to the proclamation of the gospel and is the culmination of the One-Night Revival. This is the time that is set aside to minister to the needs of the people: to the unsaved, to those that desire to be filled with the Holy Ghost, to the sick, and to those who are demon possessed or oppressed). There is no set time for this serviced to end. The Spirit of God must be given full reign to direct the service.

The Deliverance Service will conclude with a break time until 3 a.m. Before everyone is dismissed, the shut-in leader or designee will ask for four volunteers to pray for fifteen minutes each during the 3 a.m. prayer and four volunteers for the 6 a.m. prayer.

12 midnight **Prayer**

SATURDAY

3 a.m.   **Congregational Prayer:** The designated individuals pray at their appointed time. Each one immediately follows the other without comment or introduction.

4 a.m.   **Scripture Reading:** "O God, thou art my God; early will I seek thee: my soul thirsteth for thee, my flesh longeth for thee in a dry and thirsty land, where no water is; To see thy power and thy glory, so as I have seen thee in the sanctuary" (Psalms 63:1-2).

Note that only prayer and scripture reading are offered here; the message from the word of God will be offered in the next segment.

6 a.m.   **Prayer of Thanksgiving:** Let us come before his presence with thanksgiving, and make a joyful noise unto him with psalms (Psalms 95:2). This is the time of praise and thanksgiving to God for the awesome experience during the Sixty-Hour Consecration. Such prayers of thanksgiving were offered in Nehemiah 11:17: "And Mattaniah the son of Micha, the son of Zabdi, the son of Asaph, was the principal to begin the thanksgiving in prayer..." Four individuals pray for fifteen minutes each.

7 a.m.   **Scripture Reading:** Matthew 4:1-11

"Then was Jesus led up of the Spirit into the wilderness to be tempted of the devil. And when he had fasted forty days and forty nights, he was afterward an hungered. And when the tempter came to him, he said, If thou be the Son of God, command that these stones be made bread. But he answered and said, It is written, Man shall not live by bread alone, but by every word that proceedeth out of the mouth of God. Then the devil taketh him up into the holy city, and setteth him on a pinnacle of the temple, And saith unto him, If thou be the Son of God, cast thyself down: for it is written, he shall give his angels charge concerning thee: and in their hands they shall bear thee up, lest at any time thou dash thy foot against a stone.

"Jesus said unto him, It is written again, Thou shalt not tempt the Lord thy God. Again, the devil taketh him up into an exceeding high mountain, and sheweth him all the kingdoms of the world, and the glory of them; And saith unto him, All these things will I give thee, if thou wilt fall down and worship me. Then saith Jesus unto him, Get thee hence, Satan: for it is written, Thou shalt worship the Lord thy God, and him only shalt thou serve. Then the devil leaveth him, and, behold, angels came and ministered unto him."

The shut-in leader or designee will give words of encouragement and exhortation to the participants of the consecration. He or she will caution that Satan often attacks immediately after the shut-in just as he did Jesus when he had fasted 40 days and nights. If Jesus himself was tempted by the enemy then how much more should we be aware of the enemy's devices and tactics. Jesus warned in Matthew 26:41:

"Watch and pray, that ye enter not into temptation: the spirit indeed is willing, but the flesh is weak."

The Word of God: Your choice of speaker (approximately thirty minutes)

Jericho March: Our scriptural support for the Jericho March is found in the sixth chapter of Joshua. The reading of the selected passages below summarizes the story of how God chose to break down the walls of the city leading into the long awaited Promised Land.

Joshua 6:1-4, 10, 16, 20:

"Now Jericho was straitly shut up because of the children of Israel: none went out, and none came in. And the Lord said unto Joshua, See, I have given into thine hand Jericho, and the king thereof, and the mighty men of valour. And ye shall compass the city, all ye men of war, and go round about the city once. Thus shalt thou do six days. And seven priests shall bear before the ark seven trumpets of rams' horns: and the seventh day ye shall compass the city seven times, and the priests shall blow with the trumpets" (Joshua 6:1-4).

"And Joshua had commanded the people, saying, Ye shall not shout, nor make any noise with your voice, neither shall any word proceed out of your mouth, until the day I bid you shout; then shall ye shout" (verse 10).

"And it came to pass at the seventh time, when the priests blew with the trumpets, Joshua said unto the people,

Shout; for the Lord hath given you the city" (verse 16).

"So the people shouted when the priests blew with the trumpets: and it came to pass, when the people heard the sound of the trumpet, and the people shouted with a great shout, that the wall fell down flat, so that the people went up into the city, every man straight before him, and they took the city" (verse 20).

Archaeologists discovered the mound of Jericho was surrounded by a great earthen rampart, or embankment, with a stone retaining wall at its base. The retaining wall was 12–15 feet high. On top of that was a mud brick wall (six feet) thick and about 20–26 feet high.

At the crest of the embankment was a similar mud brick wall whose base was roughly 46 feet above the ground level outside the retaining wall. This is what loomed high above the Israelites as they marched around the city each day for seven days. Humanly speaking, it was heavily fortified, with a virtually unconquerable double wall, utterly impossible for the Israelites to invade.

In spite of this, a great miracle of faith happened. As they marched around the city seven times on the seventh day, the walls fell down flat and they took the city. How much more our Lord will perform a great miracle of faith as we march our walls down in victory?

The Jericho March is the culmination of the Sixty-Hour Consecration, thanking God that spiritual walls are down through the blood of the Lamb and the power of the Holy Ghost.

Marching Instructions: The shut-in leader or designee will instruct participants to line up in the center aisle of the sanctuary in pairs. It is recommended that pastors, missionaries, evangelists, other church leaders, officials of the host church and community leaders take the front positions in the march.

While all are in the center aisle in pairs, the shut-in leader will instruct each person to offer three petitions. These three petitions are given in silence and in the following order: firstly, for self; secondly, for family members or entire household; thirdly, for non-family members or entire household.

After the silent prayers, the shut-in leader or designee will request two individuals within the sanctuary to anoint each person while they are marching down the center aisle. This anointing is only done at the beginning of the march, the first time around.

The two individuals, then, will anoint each other and join the others who have marched down the center aisle. The shut-in leader and/or the designee will be responsible for counting the number of times the participants are marching around the sanctuary or the outside of the church. This depends on the size of the church and the number of people in the march. The goal is to complete seven rounds in or outside the sanctuary. Each participant is to complete:

Two times around...for yourself
Two times around...for a family member
Two times around...for a non-family member
The last time around...for thanksgiving (with a shout!)

This makes a total of seven times, the number of divine completion and spiritual victory. The Jericho March concludes with a shout and praise to God for deliverance, thanking Him that walls are broken and demolished through the power of the Holy Spirit. This is a moment of victory and praise for spiritual breakthroughs. Under this powerful moment of great praise and thankfulness, the shut-in leader will conclude the march.

In chapters 10 and 11, you will read of many miracles and breakthroughs that have occurred during this march. When the seventh round is completed, the leader will request all to return to their seats. After everyone has taken their seats, the shut-in leader or designee will ask everyone to stand and go to three persons and testify to them, saying: "My walls are down and I praise God for the victory!"

Blessing of the Oil and Handkerchiefs:
"Is any sick among you? Let him call for the elders of the church; and let them pray over

him, anointing him with oil in the name of the Lord: And the prayer of faith shall save the sick, and the Lord shall raise him up; and if he have committed sins, they shall be forgiven him" (James 5:14-15).

"So that from his body were brought unto the sick handkerchiefs or aprons, and the diseases departed from them, and the evil spirits went out of them" (Acts 19:12).

This time of blessing or prayer over the olive oil and handkerchiefs that the participants have brought to the shut-in for this purpose is in keeping with the above scriptures. For participants who do not have any handkerchiefs, pieces of white cloths may be cut up, if available. Three persons are selected to lay hands on the bottles of oil, handkerchiefs, pieces of cloths and pray over them. The three persons selected will pray separately and audibly.

Praying Over Requests in the Prayer Box:

"Be careful for nothing; but in everything by prayer and supplication with thanksgiving let your requests be made known unto God" (Philippians 4:6).
"And Hezekiah received the letter of the hand of the messengers, and read it; and Hezekiah went up into

the house of the Lord, and spread it before the Lord" (2 Kings 19:14).

Three persons are selected by the shut-in leader or designee to lift up in prayer requests that have been placed in the Prayer Box. Each person selected to pray, will pray separately that God will respond to the petitions written and submitted in the Prayer Box. These requests are not read, but they are blessed and answered through prayer. At the end of the shut-in, prayer requests are taken outside and lifted up as a burnt sacrifice unto the Lord. According to 2 Chronicles 7:1:

"Now when Solomon had made an end of praying, the fire came down from heaven, and consumed the burnt offering and the sacrifices; and the glory of the Lord filled the house."

Confirm prior to the service that the host church provides lighter/matches and an appropriate receptacle for the burning of the prayer requests.

The Word of God (about 30 minutes): This is the last spiritual meal for the shut-in. The host pastor or his/her designee will bring the message of the gospel.

Rededication of the Church: The shut-in leader or designee will read from I Kings 8:22-53, I Kings 9:1-3, and 2 Chronicles 6 and 7. The leader instructs everyone to go to various sections of the church. While the leader prays, the participants are laying hands on everything within the sanctuary that is utilized by the church for the praise and worship of God and for the edification of the people of God. Pastors or their designees will take the pulpit.

This practice during the shut-in is a reaffirmation of the presence of God ("Shekinah Glory") during the entire Sixty-Hour Consecration and a symbol of the restoration of the spiritual gifts through the means of praying and fasting in the local church. Oil is not used for this particular spiritual activity.

Sharing of Overcoming Testimonies (time permitting): Testimonies of salvation, deliverance, healing, Spirit-baptism can be shared at this time. Those that were blessed during the shut-in who would like to give their testimony of deliverance will come forth by lining up across the front of the sanctuary. The leader instructs each one to make the testimony brief.

> "And they overcame him by the blood of the Lamb, and by the word of their testimony; and they loved not their lives unto the death" (Revelation 12:11).

Remarks, Benediction, and Blessing of Food: The host church is asked to prepare soup, juice and crackers for the participants of the shut-in to break their fast. If this is your first time in the shut-in, we encourage you to eat a little soup and let it digest before eating again. The pastor and/or designee makes final remarks. A prayer of benediction is offered for safe travel and for the blessing of the food.

"Then Jesus called his disciples unto him, and said, I have compassion on the multitude, because they continue with me now three days, and have nothing to eat: and I will not send them away fasting, lest they faint in the way" (Matthew 15:32).

12 noon   **Refreshments:** The participants enjoy rich fellowship and look forward to the next shut-in.

Chapter 10

Shut-In Miracles and Rewards: Testimonies from Individuals

"And they overcame him by the blood of the Lamb and by the word of their testimony" (Revelation 12:11).

This chapter presents a selection of written testimonies of the various miracles that have occurred as a result of the shut-in revivals conducted throughout the nation since the vision of 1983. The fact that the writers have willingly used their full names and other identifying information give credence to their stories of deliverance. My purpose in sharing these breakthroughs is not to exalt the shut-in ministry or to exalt human deeds or efforts, but, rather, to glorify God for his wonder-working power. He will show Himself strong through and in those who avail themselves to him.

Healed of Arthritis

I had suffered with arthritis over 20 years, but after being prayed for in the shut-in, the Lord delivered me and I am yet healed. My mother, Mother Sallie Gilmore, became ill when

Sis. Leonard and the team were at Faith Temple in 1990. After the prayer of faith was prayed, my mother was delivered. We pray that the shut-in ministry will continue.

Alice Tyson
Evanston, IL

Healed of Impaired Sight and Fibroid Tumors

I give God praise for blessing me to attend the first shut-in with Evangelist Mamie Leonard in August, 1983. I went into the shut-in expecting healing for my eyes. At that time I was wearing bifocal glasses and had worn them for twelve years. After three days of praying and fasting before the Lord, my eyes were healed. I went to the doctor for my check-up and he confirmed that I did not need glasses any more. I give God praise. In the shut-in of January 1984, I was healed of fibroid tumors. I was scheduled to have surgery that same month. That Friday night of the shut-in during the altar call, the Lord gave Elder Prince Sykes a word of knowledge that the power of God was present to heal tumors. I immediately went down expecting my miracle. I went to the doctor for my check-up and he stated in amazement that I did not need surgery. I praise God for a confirmed healing. I thank God for Evangelist Mamie Leonard's commitment to prayer. Her life has been a blessing to many.

Evangelist Doris R. Owens
Los Angeles, CA

Restored Ability to Fast

I praise God for the Mamie Leonard Shut-In Ministry. Through this ministry, the Lord enabled me to fast again. When I became an insulin-dependent diabetic, I thought my fasting days were over. However, as I began to attend the various shut-ins, my faith increased and I began to trust God. The Lord blessed me to totally fast three days and nights without eating anything, although sometimes I did drink water. I didn't have any headaches or stomach aches. I give God all the praise for blessing me to fast again. I praise God for he is truly wonderful! Just put your trust in God, and he will meet all your needs!

Evangelist Norma J. Heard
Houston, TX

Highlights of the Goose Creek, SC Shut-In

What great joy and fulfillment it has been to me, being a part of this great end-time shut-in prayer and fasting ministry. Within the last several years, the prayer team has traveled throughout the United States. April 1988 holds many great memories for me. I was blessed to travel with this team to Goose Creek, SC; thirteen of us in number. Being unemployed at the time and having a severely sprained ankle, I sought the Lord regarding this trip. God not only gave me assurance to travel but also blessed me with $841. With my ankle in a cast, I was able to make the trip successfully. All praises to Jesus.

While en route to Goose Creek, God blessed Sis. Salter and I to meet an airline stewardess who was so moved by our sharing the shut-in ministry with her, she stated, "I need a touch from God." Because of extra time in Goose Creek she was blessed to attend the shut-in on Saturday morning. Saints traveled as far as 400 miles to attend this shut-in and stayed the entire time.

A Methodist pastor marveled over the great number of saints in prayer at 6 a.m. on Saturday morning. About 500 in attendance were awaiting the Jericho March. Due to the vast number of saints, the Jericho March was held in and outside of the church. During the Jericho March, the walls of oppression that comes to plague the saints fell down by the power of God. This service is one of the highlights of the shut-in ministry.

Evangelist Elvestine Evans
Los Angeles, CA

Restoration of Marriage

We give God praise for restoring our marriage during a shut-in revival in February 1985. I was looking forward to the shut-in, however, my husband Wesley did not feel I was making any sense wanting to stay in the church for three day and nights. His words to me were, 'I am going to check this out!' At this time our marriage was kind of shaky. We went to the shut-in and the Lord did a great thing for my husband and me. My husband came to check it out, but God checked him in. He got saved, our marriage was restored, and we united in fellowship with Love and Unity COGIC under the leadership of Pastor Ron Hill. God is yet getting the glory for this miracle of salvation and restoration.

Cheryl and Wesley Crosson
Los Angeles, CA

Multiple Miracles

Because of the shut-in ministry I was reclaimed, a daughter was reclaimed, two daughters were saved. Thus all four of my children are saved, filled with the Holy Ghost and living a committed life for Christ. I was a backslider for twenty years. A sister told me of a fasting and prayer shut-in at Mount Calvary. I went in on Thursday night. I couldn't lie down because of the coughing from smoking. God brought me into a humble and repentant heart, delivered and set me free. To this day I am still with the Lord. During these past seven years I have been healed of sickle cell. I was blessed with a home in San Bernardino, CA. I have learned how to walk by faith daily. I am now working for the Lord in Rochester, MN. The Lord has blessed me to work as an intercessory prayer evangelist. Since I left my job as an accountant in February 1988, the Lord has sustained me. Thank God for Sis. Mamie Leonard and her team for their obedience to the Lord. God bless you all. I love you dearly.

Della Cantrell
Rochester, MN

Baptized in the Holy Spirit

I was saved in February 1980, but was not baptized with the Holy Ghost until April 1984 in San Diego. I am a member of a Baptist church in Bakersfield, CA. The shut-ins have kept me with a desire to seek the more of the Lord. Through fasting, prayer and hearing the testimonies of the saints, it has encouraged me and strengthened my faith. During the shut-ins that I have been blessed to attend, I have witnessed physical healings, deliverance from drugs, alcohol and all manner of spiritual bondages. Sis. Leonard has been such a blessing because of her holiness or hell preaching. And there is no way to describe Sis. Featherston's Jericho March except to say that the Holy Spirit had his way! May God bless the shut-in ministry and all of the team.

Erma L. Nutt
Bakersfield, CA

Baptized in the Holy Spirit

It was on August 8, 1988 that I was filled with the Holy Ghost at the shut-in revival held at Antioch Temple COGIC in Panama City, FL. I had been saved for a long time and yet I knew there was something missing in my life. That was the baptism of the Holy Ghost. Thanks be to God for Sis. Mamie Leonard and the prayer and fasting shut-in team. I was invited to come to the shut-in on that Saturday morning. Coming from the Baptist church where I had been a member all of my life, we were not taught about the baptism of the Holy Ghost and yet I knew I needed something else to keep me saved. My life has not been the same. The Holy Ghost is my keeper, my help in the time of need. So this day, I thank God for his power in my life.

Minister Miriam Ruth Newsome
Panama City, FL

Healed of Brain Tumor

In 1981, I was diagnosed as having a pituitary tumor of the brain; surgery was performed. In 1982, I started having the same symptoms in my head; a second surgery was performed. The next year (1983), a group of neurologists concluded that I needed a third operation. I decided I was not going through another surgery. That's when I turned it over to the Lord. I attended the fasting and prayer shut-in where Evangelist Mamie Leonard was the leader. I was the last person in the prayer line, which was very long. She anointed my head with oil and prayed for me. In my mind I said, 'Lord, I need more.' As Evangelist Leonard tried to release her hand from my head, the Holy Spirit was so great that she was unable to completely release me. My head fell back in her hands. That night I was healed from a horrendous brain tumor—it was confirmed by my surgeon. Thank God for Evangelist Mamie Leonard. For surely, I am a miracle!

Louise Cole
Los Angeles, CA

Healed of Lesbianism and Depression

I thank God for the Mamie Leonard Shut-In Ministry because that was the setting he used to deliver me from a 30-year secret that haunted me. A shut-in was well under way in Moreno Valley, CA when an anointed woman ministering into our lives walked up to me and spoke directly into my spirit: "God wants to get into your secrets." I literally shook in my shoes and felt faint. I prayed in my spirit, "God, please don't let her tell on me in here." Denial is deadly. Shame and guilt carried a sense of torment because they are rooted in fear. My secret began as a teenager. I was lonely, insecure and confused about my sexual desires. I lost my virginity at age 12 because I was desperately trying to be accepted by my peers. I resorted to lying, stealing and manipulation to develop opportunities to carry out my fantasies. I went from promiscuity to lesbianism to bi-sexuality. The choices that I made through the age of 24 were made out of loneliness and the pain of rejection I had experienced from some young men I knew. I got married to a young man in Texas and was soon divorced. This caused me to live with another weight of shame and guilt that continued to fuel my depression. Suicidal thoughts consumed my mind.

One of my co-workers, who was a Christian woman, encouraged me to attend a Mamie Leonard shut-in so that I could be delivered from the sense of failure and shame of the divorce. I was immediately delivered from depression and burst into laughter. The joy of the Lord became my strength! Three years ago God led me to the shut-in in Moreno Valley,

CA. Evangelist Mamie Leonard exhorted us to testify about what God had done in the shut-in. I went forward thinking I would share a victory about a financial breakthrough I was believing God for, but I told my history of lesbianism. I was shocked that I said anything about that, but it was so freeing! I no longer had a secret haunting me. Depression began to be lifted from me and over time, I have learned to fight oppression and depression. The shut-in ministry team says I look more feminine now. Through prayer and fasting God has broken the soul ties that held me to sexual immorality. I thank God for the shut-in ministry.

Kathy
San Diego, CA

Healed of Fractured Spine

At age 16, I was helping my sister at her home during her first pregnancy, when I bent down to pick up something and was unable to stand back up. I had to lie on the floor on a heating pad, thinking that I pulled a muscle. I began to experience severe lower back and neck pain. When I went to the doctor, the prognosis was that I had fractured the fifth and sixth vertebrae in my neck and that they healed incorrectly, the lower portion of my spine had not developed properly and this caused my pelvis to turn three inches away from its normal position. My athletic career came to an end with the news that the doctors would either have to re-break my neck and set it properly or I would become paralyzed from an injury while playing football. For two-thirds of my life I suffered with this affliction and the pain was excruciating, I would be on the floor on my back for months at a time. Chiropractors would adjust my pelvis to get it back to its normal position and this would take time due to the swelling of the internal organ inside the pelvis cavity.

I moved to California in May 2004 and sought to get my life straight with God. My wife, who was just a friend at that time, invited me to Lighthouse Church for my first Bible study. I attended the Mamie Leonard shut-in with my back out; it had been out for a short time and was very difficult to manage. I came not really seeking healing but to get closer to God. I decided to complete the consecration fast during this time. It was hard getting up during the night for the scheduled prayer times as much as we did, but I looked forward to seeing what God was going to do and the testimonies from those God had already healed. On Saturday morning, the Jericho March around the church was incredible. I remember starting the march and the last go around the periphery of the church. As I approached the sound booth, a warm heat overtook my body starting from my head and continued through my whole body. I suddenly felt no pain and I began to jump up and down. I had not been able to do this for many years. I knew then that I was healed.

Kelvin D. Wimbush
Harbor City, CA

Fasted Without Taking Insulin

Mother Pattie Dorsey who has been on the Mother's Board at her church for approximately 10 years has also been afflicted with diabetes since 1986. She first started taking the pills for this condition and in 2004 began taking the insulin shots. She had habitually gotten used to taking the insulin shots per her physician's instructions and was afraid not to continue taking it for fear of her condition worsening. Mother Dorsey had fasted unto the Lord many times in the past and God had strengthened her through each one. However, due to the insulin shots she found herself having to gradually decrease the fasts altogether for a season. At the

2006 shut-in, Mother Dorsey was listening to Sis. Mamie Leonard's teaching about the reasons that people with afflictions say they cannot fast. She emphasized that when you have an affliction, the devil uses that infirmity to speak to your mind that you cannot fast. So when Mother Dorsey heard this teaching under the anointing of the Holy Ghost, she thought within herself, "She's speaking directly to me."

Her faith increased that the Lord would take her through this consecration, although, when Mother Dorsey came to the shut-in she only had intended to stay a few hours only and return home to be able to eat and take her insulin shots. She received the word of faith and decided to stay for the duration of the shut-in and continued fasting the entire time. In the past when Mother Dorsey would fast she would experience nausea, headaches and sometimes fever but this time she felt renewed strength and suffered no side effects. After the shut-in concluded she drove herself home and took her blood sugar test and it was 160. Hallelujah!! Mother Dorsey rejoiced in her soul because the Lord had given her endurance to go through. God had brought her to a higher level of faith in him. To God be the glory for great things he hath done.

Pattie Dorsey
Los Angeles, CA

Blessed with God-Fearing Husband

I was a single parent with three children. While struggling with many inner hurts, I kept myself and my children before the presence of God in the monthly shut-in ministry with Evangelist Mamie Leonard. I saw God bring down personal walls in many lives, most of all mine and my children. During the shut-in in Tulsa, OK, the church was illuminated in praise. Many were saved and filled with the Holy

Ghost. I have never been the same since the Tulsa shut-in, and neither has my personal ministry. I have been blessed me with a God-fearing husband and father for my children. My life has been empowered by the shut-in ministry.

Evangelist Lois Horton-Moore
Riverside, CA

Delivered from Cocaine Addiction

I came home to Los Angeles after living in Sacramento recovering from major surgery. During this time, I began to ask God where he wanted me and I desired to be more involved with him. God laid Sis. Mamie Leonard on my heart. I remembered how she was a praying woman of God and I wanted to be a part of her ministry. I began coming to prayer three days a week. Sis. Jackson and all the saints prayed for me mightily. Sis. Jackson told me to begin fasting and I did so until the year was out. I then started a new job and continued to attend Bible study every single day and church on Sundays. I also continued regular fasting. I was on crack cocaine so bad I couldn't see my way out. One day during the cold winter I was sleeping in a cold house with no lights, no gas and nowhere to take a bath. I cried out to the Lord to heal me and deliver me. I went to the Mamie Leonard shut-in and I received my deliverance that day.

Mary Hicks
Long Beach, CA

Delivered from Dependence on Prescription Drugs

In August 2005 I went to one of Mother Mamie Leonard's shut-ins and at that time I was taking 16 pills a day and was on a walker. As I went in, I asked God to heal me, to be a doctor and take me off some of the medication. God did just that. Since that time, I no longer take the pills and do not use a walker any more. I attended a subsequent shut-in, this time seeking God for finances and to cure a long-time hate. God did just that. Prayer changes things.

Beverly Watkins
San Diego, CA

Delivered from Lesbianism and Substance Abuse

I am 31 years old and have been saved for close to eight years. My mother was a heroin addict and my father was a cocaine addict. When my mother got saved, I was happy that she was no longer using drugs. However, I still had my own struggles. I drank alcohol heavily, smoked marijuana on a regular basis, hung out in different clubs, and seemed to be continually seeking for peace and something to numb my feelings. I continued to search for answers to this thing called life. All of my searching led me into a promiscuous lifestyle. By the time I was 17, I had experimented sexually with a female friend of mine. This opened the door to a whole new level of perversion in my life. Within a couple of years, I was deeply involved in a monogamous lesbian relationship that lasted for two years. Living this secret life made me absolutely sick on the inside.

Still searching for peace, and wanting to support my mom, I found myself in church more and more often. The Lord began to work on me. During this process, I attended a number of Mamie Leonard shut-ins. I remember standing in line for prayer during one of the deliverance services and petitioning the Lord for deliverance. Mother Leonard prayed fervently for me. Those shut-ins propelled me forward in my process of deliverance and enhanced my relationship with the Lord immensely. I have now been set free by the Blood of the Lamb. I thank God for how he used Mother Leonard and the shut-in team to minister to me. Today, I am an ordained elder, youth leader, and faithful member of my church. The Lord has also used me to write a book about my deliverance from lesbianism. What an absolute miracle!

Elder Autumn Bailey
San Diego, CA

Baptized with Holy Spirit

I received the Holy Ghost at a shut-in one Saturday morning. After Sis. Featherston, Mother Leonard's twin sister, had ministered to me, I went into the restroom. The Holy Ghost filled me right there in the restroom and I started praising the Lord. When I returned to the sanctuary, I gave my testimony!

Theresa Jones
Los Angeles, CA

Healed of Pain Medicine Addiction

In the 1960s, I tore the cartilage in my right leg. Due to the pain, I began taking aspirin five to fifteen times a day. When I moved to California in 1969, the physician began drawing fluid to clean my right knee. He recommended surgery but I refused. That's when the doctors told me that eventually my leg would be very uncomfortable for me. His diagnosis was correct. I became addicted to all kinds of pain pills, which included Motrin, Dorveset, Codeine, Vicodin and Ultrams. I had to combine these with over-the-counter medications to deaden the pain. Years later I had the surgery. In 1976, God saved me. I stopped taking the medicine for about six months but substituted it with aspirins. I started taking prescription drugs and continued for approximately 30 years. I needed pills to go to sleep and pills to get up in the morning. I was taking approximately 16 pills a day. Sometimes I had to double the medicine because my body had begun to reject the single dose of medicine. At night, I realized I had taken 32 pills in one day. I would be so depressed because of the struggle it was to get up during the day. I was suffering and I couldn't take it anymore. I gave up thinking that I could be delivered.

One night I was lying in bed and the Lord led me to call Sis. Jackson to ask if she still attended prayer and Bible study at Greater Deliverance COGIC in Inglewood where Mother Leonard's husband was the pastor. She said yes and volunteered to pick me up. I started going to prayer and Bible study. They announced that the upcoming shut-in would be held in Vallejo, CA. Sis. Jackson and her daughter agreed to pay for my fare so that I could attend. At Mother Leonard's shut-in they began fasting Wednesday through Saturday. Up until this time, I had only fasted for two to three hours in a day. Further, I had gone to the shut-ins time after time, and had gone without food, but not without medication. I knew I was going to take my medication with me, but God was in the plan. The closer it got to Wednesday the more fearful I became. The Lord quickened me with his word, 'God has not given us the spirit of fear...' (2 Timothy 1:7). Every time the fear came over me I would repeat this verse.

I started my fast that Wednesday night. Being diabetic and knowing the condition was out of control, I deliberately left all the medicine at home. God took me through those three days of the shut-in. I was sick on the second day. I laid down a lot because my body began to ache, but God saw me through. I heard one of the saints quote the scripture: 'As they went they were healed.' I grabbed hold of faith in God's word and for about six months I counted each day I went without medication. It was a great feeling of joy not taking medicine for five years after thirty years of addiction. I thank God for Mother Leonard hearing the call of God and most of all obeying God. God had me in his plan. The very next shut-in I attended, I experienced God's power, his love, his peace and his joy. In that same shut-in I thought I would bring my diabetes medicine and a sandwich in case I got sick. When I got to the altar for prayer, I decided to give the medicine and sandwich to Mother Leonard. She gave it back and said, "You keep it." Mother Leonard believed that I could do it. I didn't believe I could do it, but God quickened me with his word, "But let him ask in faith, nothing wavering. For he that wavereth is like a wave of the sea driven with the wind and tossed. For let not that man think that he shall receive any thing of the Lord. A double-minded man is unstable in all his ways" (James 1:6-8).

God took me through. When we got to the Jericho March I didn't feel like I could do it. But oh, what an experience that was! I felt joy, peace and deliverance. I danced in the Lord like I had never done in over twenty years since I've been saved. I had so much energy and joy in my body, although I had no food and medication. The joy of the Lord is our strength. I experienced the joy of the Lord for myself during the march. After 29 years of pain medication addiction, God delivered me. I am learning to stay in the word of God, to pray, fast, and seek God.

Ruth August
Los Angeles, CA

Abortion Averted

All my life I have been in the church so I knew that the decision I was about to make was wrong but I could not see any other way out. I was pregnant and I was going to get an abortion. I called my doctor and scheduled to have my pregnancy terminated. My mind was made up. On the way to the hospital, I made several attempts to call my mom, but she did not answer. Finally on my last try she answered her cell phone with a low whisper. "Hello." I could hear the saints in the background and I said to myself, "Oh yeah, she's at church." Once I heard her voice I wanted her to say something that would make everything okay. However, she rushed me off the phone. She said, "Juanita. if you want to talk to me come to the shut in." I really did not want to go to the hospital without talking with my mom so I went to the shut-in.

It seems as if the saints were just waiting for me, because as I walked in Sis. Mia was sharing a powerful testimony. I really started listening to what she was saying. After she finished, Mother Leonard got up and the saints were praising God. I started feeling something and I knew that if I did not leave now it would be too late. At that moment, Sis. René asked Mother Leonard to pray for me. Mother Leonard pulled out the chair and before I knew it I was up in front of the church telling my entire story of how I was on my way to have an abortion. The saints prayed for me, ministered to me and loved me. I cried as I had never before. I repented before God and promised that I would do my unborn baby no harm. I am now six months pregnant with a healthy baby boy. I won't say that everything is easy but I am so thankful to God that I did not have an abortion. I know that God will help me to raise my three sons. I am so grateful for Mother Leonard and the shut in ministry.

Juanita J. Jackson
Long Beach, CA

Increased Passion for God

After being saved for about 20 years, I finally had my first experience of spending full time in a shut-in. I did not know what to expect but I listened intently to every word that was being spoken. I know I died the first day because by Friday I was not focused on eating; I was totally caught up in what I was experiencing. I can't explain when it happened but God begin to minister to me. Every song, every testimony, every prayer had an effect on me. During the rest periods I could barely sleep because I wanted to experience more. On Friday night during the deliverance service, I was awed by the powerful move of God. We praised God until 1 a.m. I was so full I thought I was going to pop. Oh, but little did I know that the Jericho March was coming on Saturday morning. The atmosphere was charged with faith. Everyone was on one accord. I knew that God heard everyone one of my prayer requests. I can honestly say that I have never been the same since that first shut in experience, and my desire has been for the more of God and his will for my life."

Sis. Jacquelyn Davis
Ontario, CA

Sickle Cell Free

In my early years as a child, I would have severe pains in my legs and arms and my parents never knew what was wrong with me. They would take me to the doctor and he would say I must have sprained an arm or leg and wrap me in bandages. My aunt advised my mother that I should see a blood specialist because her son had sickle cell anemia and shared my symptoms. My parents took her advice and they too got tested. My mom and dad had no idea that both of them had the trait which resulted in me having sickle cell anemia.

I went through my childhood life with severe pain for days at a time. There were many times that I was taken out of school to recover from my crisis. In 1987 at the age of 10, I went through one of the worst crisis I had ever experienced. I had to be hospitalized and given blood. My uncle was a pastor within the Church of God In Christ in Tallahassee, FL. He asked my parents to bring me to his church for a shut-in that he was having for a three-day weekend. My parents were reluctant at the time to travel with me because I was still very ill. My mother decided she would bring me there after the doctor released me from the hospital. We drove up on a Thursday night and went straight to the church. My mother brought all of my medicines and liquids that my doctor said I must take for the next few weeks in order to fully recover. I stayed in the back of the church and my mother and relatives would take turns monitoring me.

Although I was only 10, I was tired of being sick. I asked my mom and dad several times in the past, why did I have this disease and my other friends could play and participate in activities that I couldn't do. They would explain to me how precious I was to God and how he doesn't allow things to happen to us if he wasn't going to get the glory from it. While the church was praying and crying out to God all night Thursday night and Friday, I would lay there and cry and pray too. I asked God to heal my body and make me "normal" like other kids. My mom would feed me and give me Gatorade and water even though everyone else there was fasting. She wanted me to get my strength back.

Saturday morning service was the last day of the Shut In. I remained in the back with my mother while service continued. Mamie and Martha asked my mother could they pray for me and she said of course. They laid their hands on me and begin to anoint my body with oil. I cried because I was sincere in asking God to heal my body. They asked me if I felt like walking and I said yes. We begin walking around the walls in the back of the church as they continued to pray. We then walked along the side of the church towards the front and I past out under the anointing. Someone must have laid me down on the front pew because when I woke up, that is were I was lying. As I begin to wake up, I was uttering in tongues! Someone put a microphone to my mouth and the tongues begin to rumble through me and out of my mouth. It was unbelievable! The church began praising God and the Holy Spirit filled the room. I got up off the seat, with no pain! It was like I was in a daze. I couldn't believe what was happening and Martha asked me where the pain was? I cried and said "Nowhere!" I am now 30 years old and still sickle cell free! What an awesome God we serve.

Erica Alexander
Jacksonville, FL

Blessing to Me and My Family

Thank God for you, Sis. Mamie, for obeying God. The shut-in ministry has been a blessing to me and my family. In 1984, God blessed the doors to be opened at Linda Vista Second Baptist Church. It was one of the best shut-ins ever. The Lord filled me with the Holy Ghost in that shut-in. I have learned how to fast and pray, now God has given me a ministry in my home. We meet every Thursday night for Bible study. The women are saved and filled with the Holy Ghost. The Lord also blessed my husband during the shut-in. He was delivered from smoking and drinking. Keep the shut-in going, Sis. Mamie. It has been a blessing to many people.

Sis. Ann Langston
San Diego, CA

Turned Their Lives Around

I first heard of the shut-in ministry in December 1983. I have followed the ministry since January 1984. I have seen many people blessed, delivered, and baptized with the Holy Ghost. God has blessed me to set up a religious non-profit corporation ministering to the spiritual, emotional, and physical needs of men and women whose commitment is to turn their lives around after hearing the word of God while in prison. We have a one-year program to teach self-esteem and family values, and to help establish each resident in God's word before they return to the community. Thank you for the inspiration.

Sis. Ruthie Gray
Los Angeles, CA

Chapter 11

Shut-In Miracles and Rewards: Testimonies from Spiritual Leaders

The goal of the shut-in ministry is to encourage individuals to seek God through corporate prayer and fasting, and to encourage pastors and other church leaders to make opportunities available for people to pursue and embrace these spiritual disciplines. The shut-in ministry has crisscrossed the nation impacting individuals and churches alike.

The testimonies below, submitted by the shut-in team, pastors, and other spiritual leaders will inspire your faith and increase your hunger for a move of God.

Passed a Tumor

Sis. Mamie Leonard approached me in 1983 and asked me to assist her in conducting the prayer and fasting shut-in ministry. The first shut-in was at Mt. Calvary Church of God in Christ. I have many fond memories of how God saved, filled with the Holy Spirit, and healed many sick people.

I particularly remember a lady who went to the ladies' room and passed a tumor. I was blessed by the many times we prayed for all pastors, and especially for the pastors who had members participating in the shut-in. I will forever be grateful for the spiritual benefits that I received from being a part of the shut-in ministry. I have found prayer and fasting to be a major key to the success of the ministry that God has given me.

May God continue to bless Sis. Mamie Leonard for her commitment and dedication to the prayer and fasting shut-in.

Pastor Ron Hill
Love and Unity COGIC
Compton, CA

Breakthrough and Anointing

We first learned of your ministry through West Angeles COGIC. We felt led to attend this "shut-in." We had never heard of a shut-in or attended one. The Lord truly blessed us. On Saturday morning, Sis. Mamie Leonard along with Sis. Martha Featherston led us in a Jericho March. It was awesome! Breakthrough and the anointing of God were there in a powerful way. Since that first shut-in, the Lord has partnered us together to have Sis. Mamie work with us and hold prayer shut-ins at Angeles Temple and Union Presbyterian Church as part of events we convened. The prayer and fasting ministry produces results and miracles for those who join in.

Elder Fred and Wilma Berry
Azusa Street Mission and Historical Society
Los Angeles, CA

Personal Encounter

It is really hard to find words sufficient enough to describe the impact that the Mamie Leonard Shut-In Ministry has had on my life and the St. Luke Church family as a whole. What we witnessed during both of the shut-ins was nothing short of a miraculous, Holy Spirit, divine anointing in a powerful way. Our minds were enlightened, our spirits edified, our hearts encouraged, and our determination strengthened. There was a genuine manifestation of the word. It came to life before our eyes as each one received a blessing from a personal encounter with the Lord. During the hours of prayer, the shekinah glory of the Lord was present.

There were several that were healed, restored and delivered, and all were strengthened in their spirits and from the love that was shed among the saints. We experienced genuine fellowship within the body of Christ, even though there was individuals present who had never met one another before. That did not hinder nor restrain individuals from participating and grabbing hold of the flow of the anointing that was in the place. The teaching was superb and the Friday night camp-style meeting was explosive. I believe my personal favorite was the Jericho March where I witnessed individuals slain in the Spirit and their personal walls coming down. Glory to God!

Pastors James and Liz Patton
St. Luke Baptist Church
Arcadia, LA

Whole Church in Prayer

While endeavoring to lead the congregation at West Adams to a greater prayer emphasis I became informed of the Mamie Leonard Shut-In Ministry. This appeared to be such an innovative way of incorporating the whole church in prayer that I eagerly obtained the approval of the senior pastor and we had our first prayer shut-in in 1987. What impressed me most about these fasting and prayer shut-ins was the method of around-the-clock scheduling the time into separate hours of exhortation, prayer, and rest/meditation. This provided adequate time for both instruction and effectual prayer, and then putting it into practice. It is like a second hand to the local pastor in praying for specific needs of his or her congregation and also of the community. Fasting and praying marked the growth and success of the early church and I am convinced it is the one remaining ingredient needed for today—a great need for renewal. I pray that this ministry will continue on and on and expand way beyond its present border.

Rev. Martha Bagley
West Adams Foursquare Church
Los Angeles, CA

Blind Woman Healed

I am still excited about the shut-ins. The first shut-in at our church was so powerful with miracles of healing, testimonies of blessings, and people stayed in prayer who had not prayed for such a length of time. There were some diabetics who were able to fast and pray the entire time without food and insulin–and no diabetic attacks. There was a lady in the prayer who couldn't reach her arms behind her, but was able to do it by the end of the Jericho March on Saturday morning. The first shut-in was so fantastic that the following year our pastor, Elder Nathaniel Witcher, asked the prayer team to return to Providence, RI.

There was a pastor who traveled many miles out of Massachusetts and brought many of his congregation. Along came a blind lady and she didn't tell anyone that she was blind. However, she sat praying and her church family knew that she was blind. Suddenly, she jumped up during the Jericho March on Saturday morning praising God and yelling, "I can see! I can see!" over and over again. Evangelist Leonard asked her, "How blind were you?" The woman said. "I can see you for the first time and you are wearing a yellow blouse." After that the church was very sincere in continuing in prayer.

Evangelist Lyda Garvin
Pentecostal COGIC
Providence, RI

Witch Doctor Delivered

Once when Sis. Leonard was conducting a shut-in in Jamaica, a witch doctor came into the service. We were unaware of his being present, but the people seemed to get unsettled. He positioned himself in the prayer line and commenced to try and charm Sis. Leonard. The pastor of the church came behind him and put his hand on his shoulder and the man went into a rage. Sis. Leonard started binding the devil and the man settled down. He kept saying incantations. She commanded him, "Say what I say in Jesus' name!" He began to repeat after her. He became calm as he started calling the name of Jesus. The Lord delivered him! The saints begin to rejoice and run all over the place because this man had often come in and created havoc and it would take them days to put the church back together.

Submitted by shut-in team member Lenonda Robinson

Priestess Delivered

We were in a shut in at Elder Julius Rodgers' church in Los Angeles when a young lady ran into the service and said she was not leaving until she got deliverance. She was being trained to be a priestess and had gone through most of the rituals. She could not sleep for hearing the voices calling her to complete the process–which was to drink human blood. Sis. Leonard and others begin to pray and her deliverance came. When she expressed that she felt free and empty, Sis. Leonard told her that she needed the Holy Ghost to fill that void. As she tarried, it was not long before she received the gift of the Holy Ghost. She stayed the entire time of the consecration and left a new person in Christ. When her husband came to pick her up, he told her she looked different.

Submitted by shut-in team member Lenonda Robinson

Delivered From Suicide

In Tucson, AZ a woman was passing the church where the shut-in was being held and felt compelled to come in. It was at the time we were having the Prayer of Confession so she was paired with a prayer partner. She confessed that she was on her way to commit suicide. She had been crying out to God for help not knowing that help was there. Obviously she was not prepared to stay in the church but found herself remaining until the Shut-In was over that Saturday. God delivered her and set her free. When we returned to the church two-years later, she came to the shut-in. She had maintained her victory!

Submitted by shut-in team member Lenonda Robinson

No More Pain

I am reaping the benefits of that first shut-in I attended over 20 years ago. I am 85 years old and, yes, the storms keep on coming, but because of the experience of the shut-in, I am enjoying victorious living. My husband and I hosted a Mamie Leonard shut-in revival at Logan Temple AME Zion Church in the 1980s. We were determined to attend the shut-in, even-though I had oral surgery prior to this event. By the time we entered the church, I was in horrific pain and literally eating pain pills. During the deliverance service, Sis. Leonard prayed for me and I was completely healed. Logan Temple AME Zion remained committed to praying and fasting, which brought tremendous spiritual growth to the ministry of the church. Through that first shut-in, Logan AME Zion connected with the twin ministry of Martha Featherston. The church has been blessed by the experience of the Sixty-Hour Consecration.

Rev. Aaron Moore
Presiding Elder
African Methodist Episcopal Zion Church
San Diego District

Three Days of Heaven

The Mamie Leonard Shut-In Ministry was at our church in February 1990. The members are still talking of the tremendous blessing we received. It was three days of heaven on earth.

Pastor D.J. Rodgers
House of Refuge COGIC
Los Angeles, CA

Healed of Cancer

I received the Holy Ghost in a shut-in in Crossett, Arkansas in 1995. In January 1997, I was diagnosed with prostate cancer. On the same day that I was scheduled for surgery, I returned to Crossett where Mamie Leonard was conducting another shut-in. During the Deliverance Service, I went up for healing. I believed and received. Every three or four months I had a checkup. My PSA is 0.0. I thank God for my healing and I thank God for Mamie Leonard Ministries. In June 2005, I had dizziness and my walk was unbalanced. It went in for a checkup and the doctor prescribed several tests. I was diagnosed with a brain tumor. Again, I called both Mamie Leonard and her twin sister Martha Featherston for prayer. On October 6, 2005, God turned my tumor around so that surgery was made easy. The doctor was able to go through my nose and completely remove that brain tumor. I shall not die, but live and declare the works of the Lord.

Pastor Roy Murray
Liberty Hill CME Church
Ringgold, LA

Entire Church Revived

We, the pastors and members of the New Life Holiness Church, give thanks to the Lord for the Mamie Leonard shut-in that was conducted at our church from September 14-16, 1989. During this meeting, the entire church was revived, and the Lord delivered a number of people from the power of drugs. Many of the saints testified of physical healings through the power of prayer and fasting. We feel that the Lord has said to this ministry, "Well done!"

Bishop T. E. and Elzena Medlock
New Life Holiness Church
Pasadena, CA

Backsliders Reclaimed

It was indeed a great privilege, as well as a pleasure, to host you and your co-workers at Greater Open Door COGIC in October 1989 for the three-day shut-in Consecration. In that meeting God richly blessed our church and my ministry. Backsliders were reclaimed and many souls from other denominational churches were filled with the Holy Ghost. Among the backsliders was my youngest daughter. Need I say more? But then there was another amazing thing that God did in the shut-in; it happened about 6:30 a.m., Saturday morning. Two backsliders came in off the street—a young lady and her male friend. She was addicted to marijuana and he was addicted to cocaine. Because of the outpouring of the Holy Spirit, God miraculously reclaimed these two people. She became a member of Open Door and yet remains faithful. Praise God! The shut-in also gave birth to new visions. Several new prayer ministries at our church have developed and the people are encouraged to fully support the work of the church. Since the shut-in, our church has been motivated to have monthly shut-ins, weekly prayer meetings. and an intercessory group that fasts and prays.

Elder Garon Harden
Greater Open Door COGIC
Long Beach, CA

A Time of Renewal

It is truly with joy that we reflect on the two special shut-ins that we were privileged to have at West Adams Foursquare

Church, conducted by Mamie Leonard in November 1985
and 1987. How the Holy Spirit moved in our individual lives
and corporately. It was a time not to be forgotten—a time of
renewal and refreshing! Sis. Leonard opened up to us a new
way of a shut-in pattern, times of prayer, then times of medi-
tation every three hours around the clock. This is a pattern
we have now adopted at West Adams Foursquare Church for
our monthly one-day shut-in and it has proven to be a fruitful
method to follow. We wish to express our deep appreciation
to Mamie for having answered the call of God in conducting
these precious shut-ins here in Los Angeles and around the
country. Our prayer is that God may richly bless Mamie for
her faithfulness in following God's plan.

Drs. Marvin and Juanita Smith
Former Senior Pastors
West Adams Foursquare Church
Los Angeles, CA

A New Direction

We want to share with you what the Lord revealed to
us along with your vision of the shut-in ministry. He spoke
and said, "This will mark the changing of ministry; no more
evangelistic revivals, but a new direction and ministry."
Praise God for your obedience and perseverance. Hundreds
have been blessed and will continue to be changed through
your prayer ministry.

Evangelists Renee Stewart and Aretha Christopher
Youth Explosion Ministry, Inc.
Dallas, TX

Direction From God

I have found the shut-in ministry conducted by Sis. Mamie Leonard to be one of the greatest tools God is using to manifest his glory in these last days. Several days ago we were in a dilemma about whether we should begin a church to minister to the lost sheep that kept crossing our path. We found ourselves counseling and advising drug addicts, alcoholics, prostitutes, ex-offenders, and others in like situations. They were the sheep without a shepherd. More and more we were feeling that God was leading us to find a place for assembly. But, we had to be sure. So we went to the shut-in being conducted in Pasadena to seek direction from God. We met Sis. Leonard in the foyer and shared our petition with her. In the spirit of wisdom, she encouraged us to do what we were feeling led to do. She assured us that God would be with us and that he would bless the work of our hands. That was in 1995. In the past eleven years we have seen miracles, signs and wonders. People have been delivered from drugs, alcohol, homosexuality and all kinds of deviant lifestyles. God is saving the lost, healing the sick and filling with the Holy Ghost. We thank God for Mamie Leonard, his dedicated servant, and her anointed ministry team.

Pastors James and Hazel Dawson
Fellowship of Love Divine
San Diego, CA

Epilogue

I pray that the inspiring testimonies, miracles, Bible teaching on fasting, and shut-in guidance discussed in the preceding chapters have caused you to desire more of God and his presence. In a time when a great falling away is occurring throughout the church body, the ministry of a prayer and fasting shut-in revival is a powerful tool for ushering in spiritual renewal for congregations and individuals.

As we look to the Lord, let us faithfully apply the disciplines of corporate fasting and praying and thereby restore God's power in the church. We have a charge to keep and we must do it with all diligence. The will of God will be done in our lives...if we fast, pray and obey.

Appendix A

Shut-In Revival Agenda

The sixty-hour schedule set forth below is a general guide for the shut-in revival. It may be modified as needed to accommodate the size of the gathering or any other logistical issues.

WEDNESDAY

12 midnight	Fast begins in each participant's home

THURSDAY

8 p.m.	Beginning of the Shut-In: Participants Enter the House of God
9 p.m.	One-Hour Prayer
10 p.m.	Songs of Praise
	Scripture Reading: 2 Chronicles 20:1-30 and Daniel 9:3
	Teaching on How to Seek the Lord
12 midnight	Prayer of Agreement: Matthew 18:19-20

FRIDAY

1 a.m.	Break: Sleeping, Resting, Reading, Quiet Time
3 a.m.	Congregational Prayer Scripture Reading: Isaiah 58
4 a.m.	Break: Sleeping, Resting, Reading, Quiet Time
6 a.m.	Paul and Silas Prayer: Acts 16:25-26
7 a.m.	Scripture Reading: Joel 2 Teaching on the Anointing Anointing Service
9 a.m.	Prayer Walk
10 a.m.	Scripture Reading: Matthew 17:14-12 The Word of God (mini-message)
11 a.m.	Break: Sleeping, Resting, Reading, Quiet Time
12 noon	Prayer of Confession
1 p.m.	Scripture Reading The Word of God (mini-message)
1:30 p.m.	Break: Sleeping, Resting, Reading, Quiet Time
3 p.m.	One-Hour Prayer for Those in Authority
4 p.m.	Scripture Reading The Word of God (mini-message) Request four volunteers to lead 7 p.m. prayer
4:30 p.m.	Break: Sleeping, Resting, Reading, Quiet Time
7 p.m.	One-Hour Prayer (start of the One-Night Revival)
8 p.m.	Scripture Search Praise and Worship Overcoming Testimonies

	Congregational Song
9 p.m.	Circle Prayer (groups of five or six)
	Musical Selection
	Prayer for Pastors and Churches
	Free-Will Offering
	Musical Selection
	Message from the Word of God
	Deliverance Service
12 midnight	Prayer

SATURDAY

3 a.m.	One-Hour Congregational Prayer
4 a.m.	Scripture Reading
	Break: Sleeping, Resting, Reading, Quiet Time
6 a.m.	One-Hour Prayer of Thanksgiving (four people praying for about 15 minutes each)
7 a.m.	Scripture Reading: Matthew 17; Luke. 4:1-15
	Message from the Word of God (church pastor or designee)
	Jericho March: Josh. 6:1-3, 10, 16, 20
	Blessing of the Oil: James 5:14-15
	Intercession Over the Prayer Box Requests
	Re-dedication of the Host Church
	Time of Sharing: Overcoming Testimonies
	Remarks/Benediction/Blessing of Food
12 noon	Refreshments (Breaking of the fast: juice, fruits, soups)

137

Appendix B

Intercession Categories for Corporate Prayer

Government Leaders

United Nations
World leaders
President of the United States
Vice President of the United States
Secretary of State and other cabinet members
Attorney General
Congress
Central Intelligence Agency (CIA)
Federal Bureau of Investigation (FBI)
Homeland Security Agency
Chairman of the Federal Reserve Bank
Governors
State legislature
Mayors
City Council
Other government officials

Spiritual Leaders

Presiding heads of all denominations
Bishops and overseers
Mothers, elders, pastors, evangelists
Missionaries, teachers, chaplains
Church administrators
Other leaders and their families
Christian relief organizations

Armed Forces

Military leaders
Commanding officers
Deployed soldiers and their families

Justice System

Supreme Court justices
Federal, state and local judges
Lawyers

Peace and Safety Officers

Police Department
Fire Department
Firemen
Police officers
Probation officers
Prison guards
Prison ministries
Protection inside prison
Prison and penal system
Lawyers

Educational System

School boards
Principals
Teachers
Counselors
School security officers
Colleges/Universities
Prison and juvenile hall educational systems

Medical Professionals

Doctors/Surgeons
Nurses/Aides
Anesthesiologists
Nurse practitioners
Physician assistants
Pharmacists/Others

Family Authorities

Husbands/Fathers
Wives/Mothers
Grandparents
Foster Parents/Adoptive Parents

Financial and Other Institutions

Banks
Corporate chief executive officers

Appendix C

Biblical References
for Prayer and Fasting

Old Testament

Exodus 34:28
Deuteronomy 9:18
Judges 20:26
1 Samuel 7:6 / 31:13
2 Samuel 1:12 / 12:16-22
1 Kings 21:27
1 Chronicles 10:12
2 Chronicles 6:4-5 / 20:3
Ezra 8:21-23 / 10:6
Nehemiah 1:4 / 9:1-4
Esther 4:15-17
Psalms 69:9-10 / 109:24
Isaiah 37:1-3 / 58:3-7
Jeremiah 36:6-9
Daniel 6:18 / 9:3-18 / 10:1-3
Zechariah 8:19
Joel 1:13-14 / 2:3

New Testament

Matthew 4:1-2 / 6:16-18 / 9:14-15
Mark 1:12-13 / 2:18-20 / 9:29
Luke 2:37 / 4:1-2 / 5:33
Acts 9:9 / 10:30 / 13:2
2 Corinthians 11:27

Appendix D

More Testimonies
from Youths and Adults

The Mamie Leonard Shut-In Ministry has impacted people from all ages, genders, denominations and cultures. Here is a sampling of more testimonies by age:

"I am addicted to the shut-in." – *Horenea, 31*

"One of the greatest things!" – *Lean, 89*

"A great asset for those expecting a miracle and healing."
 – *Mayada, 34*

"The shut-in has been life changing for me." – *LaVett, 44*

"The shut-in is a refuge for me." – *Frances, 72*

"A life changing experience, something I will never forget."
 – *Leah, 19*

"A place to be for healing, deliverance, and a move of the Holy Spirit!!" – *Rachel, 21*

"I thank God for the joy, peace, and restoration I received in the shut-in." – *Gail, 35*

"Over the years it has been a school of learning, Holy Ghost teaching, healing, and deliverance, I've been blessed." – *Evangelist Jackson, 62*

"Awesome, dynamic, encouraging, powerful, delivering, and inspirational ministry." – *Pastor Cloud*

"A spiritual experience that I haven't received any place else." – *Lucille, 68*

"Truly burden removing and yoke breaking!" – *De Shaune, 37*

"The shut-in has and will always be a powerful and mighty manifestation of the move of God." – *Damia, 27*

"I have never experienced the Lord in the way that I have in the shut-in." – *Deshona, 19*

"God answered my prayer and He restored my relationship with Him." – *Natalie, 16*

"The testimonies given at the shut-in increased my faith" – *Jason, 11*

"The shut-in blessed me greatly because it brought me closer to God!" – *Cedric, 13*

"My hunger for God was fulfilled and increased." – *Crystal, 19*

"The experience of the Jericho Victory March blessed me."
— *Rosie, 67*

"The messages are encouraging to my soul." — *Bernadette, 47*

"It was a turning point in my spiritual walk and I've never been the same." — *Naomi, 48*

Appendix E

List of Shut-In Host Churches

The following is a partial list of churches that have hosted a shut-in revival since the inception of the ministry:

Abundant Life Tabernacle
Baton Rouge, LA
Bishop T.S. Abernathy III

All Nations Pentecostal Center COGIC
Aurora, CO
Bishop Phillip H. Porter, Pastor

Antioch COGIC
Vallejo, CA
Elder Freddie Miller, Pastor

Antioch Temple COGIC
Panama City, FL
Elder John Gipson, Pastor

Bethel Miracle COGIC
North Long Beach, CA
Elder William Hundley, Sr., Pastor

Boone Tabernacle COGIC
Kansas City, MO
Elder Floyd H. Thuston, Pastor

Breakthrough COGIC
Moreno Valley, CA
Elder Charles Gibson, Pastor

Calvary Evangelist Center
Tucson, AZ
Maynard Weisbrod, Pastor

Cedar Grove Baptist Church
Los Angeles, CA
Rev. A.T. Williams, Jr., Pastor

Christ Memorial COGIC
Pacoima, CA
Bishop Benjamin J. Crouch, Sr., Pastor

Christ Temple COGIC
Lubbock, TX
Supt. David Haynes, Pastor

Christian Faith Center Assembly of God
San Diego, CA
Elder Jerry Bernard, Pastor

Church of God Pentecostal
Inglewood, CA
Bishop Johnny Young, Pastor

Church of Rehoboth World Outreach Center
Vallejo, CA
Elder P. Daniel Jefferson, Pastor

Community Baptist Church
San Diego, CA
Rev. Claude Eugene, Jr., Pastor

Corinthian Temple COGIC
Chicago, IL
Bishop Bennie Allison, Pastor

Cornerstone Community COGIC
Marin City, CA
Johnathan Logan, Pastor

Daniels Memorial COGIC
Portland, OR
Harry Daniels, Jr., Pastor

Davis Memorial COGIC
Crossett, AK
Bishop R.E. Matheney, Pastor

Eastside Church of God in Christ
San Jose, CA
Elder Sherman Harris, Pastor

Emmanuel COGIC
Los Angeles, CA
Elder Leroy Mardis, Pastor

Ephesians COGIC
Los Angeles, CA
Elder E.E. Cleveland, Pastor

Faith Chapel COGIC
San Diego, CA
Bishop Roy L. Dixon, Pastor

Faith Tabernacle COGIC
San Diego, CA
Elder James L. Ewings, Pastor

Faith Temple COGIC
Evanston, IL
Bishop Carlis Moody, Pastor

Faith Temple COGIC
Los Angeles, CA
Elder Mack N. Trimble, Pastor

First Church of God
Inglewood, CA
Bishop Gregory Dixon, Pastor

First Foursquare Church
Compton, CA
Elder Payn Levia, Pastor

Forty-Seventh Street Church of God
San Diego, CA
Rev. Harvey L. Warren, Sr., Pastor

Fountain of Life COGIC
Banning, CA
Carlton Anderson, Pastor

Fountain of Life COGIC
Los Angeles, CA
Superintendant Isom McCray, Pastor

Friendly COGIC
Oceanside, CA
Thomas Hammond, Pastor

Friendship Baptist Church
Pasadena, CA
Elder Stanley Lewis, Pastor

Good Samaritan COGIC
San Diego, CA
Bishop Henry Mitchell, Pastor

Gospel Memorial COGIC
Long Beach, CA
Elder Joe Ealey, Pastor

Greater Harvest Ministries
Quincy, FL
Dr. Gerald Thomas, Pastor

Greater Open Door COGIC
Long Beach, CA
Elder Garon Harden, Pastor

Greater Page Temple COGIC
Los Angeles, CA
Elder Theodis Johnson, Pastor

Greater Trinity COGIC
Little Rock, AZ
Elder Saint DeWitt Hill, Pastor

Hebrew Baptist Church
Ringgold, LA
Rev. Huey P. Roberson, Pastor

Higher Dimensions Church
Tulsa, OK
Bishop Carlton Pearson, Pastor

Hillside Tabernacle COGIC
Altadena, CA
Evang. Francis Harris, Pastor

Holy Assembly COGIC
Pasadena, CA
Bishop F. J. Goodman, Pastor

House of Refuge COGIC
Los Angeles, CA
Elder Julius Rogers, Pastor

Hull Avenue COGIC
Madera, CA
Elder Dolphus McAlister, Pastor

Jackson Memorial COGIC
San Diego, CA
Bishop J.A. Blake, Sr., Pastor

Liberty COGIC
Los Angeles, CA
Bishop Henry Tyler, Pastor

Lighthouse COGIC
Long Beach, CA
Elder Samuel Jones, Pastor

Lilly of the Valley COGIC
Long Beach, CA
Elder James Shaw, Pastor

Linda Vista 2nd Baptist
San Diego, CA
Elder Robert Whitaker, Pastor

Logan Temple A.M.E. Zion Church
San Diego, CA
Dr. Howard E. Haggler, Pastor

Love and Unity COGIC
Compton, CA
Elder Ron Hill, Pastor

Manna Missionary Baptist Church
San Bernardino, CA
Rev. C. George, Jr., Pastor

Maranatha Christian Center
San Jose, CA
Dr. Tony Williams, Pastor

Metropolitan Ecclesiastical Jurisdiction
Los Angeles, CA
Bishop J. Bernard Hackworth

Modesto Christian Center
Modesto, CA
Dr. Jesse Stovall, Pastor

Mount Calvary COGIC
Los Angeles, CA
Elder Clarence Church, Jr., Pastor

Mount Olive COGIC
San Diego, CA
Elder Vernon Cooper, Pastor

Mt. Olive COGIC
Los Angeles, CA
Elder Samuel Morgan, Pastor

New Birth Apostolic Christian Church
Inglewood, CA
Bishop Ralph Artiaga, Pastor

New Gethsemane COGIC
Pomona, CA
Bishop Raymond Watts, Pastor

New Jerusalem Community
Long Beach, CA
Supt. Willie Pearce, Pastor

New Jerusalem, COGIC
Compton, CA
Elder J.T. Jones, Pastor

New Jerusalem COGIC
Tacoma, WA
Bishop T. Westbrook, Pastor

New Life COGIC
Harvey, IL
Supt. Leroy Jones, Sr., Pastor

New Life Foursquare
Los Angeles, CA
Elder Lamont Leonard, Pastor

New Life Holiness Church
Pasadena, CA
Bishop and Mrs. Thomas Medlock, Pastors

Normandie Community COGIC
Los Angeles, CA
Elder Lazell L. Rodgers, Pastor

Old Path Miracle Cathedral COGIC
Vallejo, CA
Supt. Harold Johnson, Pastor

Open Door Outreach Ministries COGIC
St. Louis, MO
Elder Jeremiah R. Grimes, Pastor

Palm Lane COGIC
Los Angeles, CA
Elder Ray Hawkins, Sr., Pastor

Pentecostal COGIC
Providence, RI
Elder Nathaniel V. Witcher, Pastor

Pentecostal Temple COGIC
Pensacola, FL
Bishop John D. Young, Sr., Pastor

Philadelphia Faith Temple COGIC
Compton, CA
Elder Wilbur McNair, Pastor

Praise Fellowship COGIC
Mishawaka, IN
Travis Bush, Pastor

Prayer Assembly COGIC
Phoenix, AZ
Edward Carter, Pastor

Progressive COGIC
Sacramento, CA
Supt. J.E. Copeland, Pastor

Revival Center Tried Stone COGIC
Los Angeles, CA
Dr. Joseph W. Mayfield, Pastor

Revival Time COGIC
Compton, CA
Elder Charles Bennett, Pastor

Richmond Vale Baptist Church
St. Thomas, Jamaica
Elder J.J. Williams, Pastor

Rock of the Valley COGIC
Van Nuys, CA
Elder James Purdom, Jr., Pastor

Saints Community COGIC
Fresno, CA
Elder Bruce E. McAlister, Pastor

Shackleford Miracle Temple COGIC
Los Angeles, CA
Elder Charles Smith, Pastor

COGIC South Carolina Jurisdiction
Bishop Johnny Jones Johnson
Mother Willie Mae Rivers, Coordinator

Southern Baptist Church
Brooklyn, NY
Rev. Clarence Williams, Pastor

St. Luke Baptist Church
Arcadia, LA
James E. and Liza Patton, Pastors

St. Luke COGIC
San Diego, CA
Supt. Gary Watkins, Pastor

St. Stephens COGIC
San Diego, CA
Bishop George D. McKinney, Pastor

Star of Bethlehem COGIC
Washington, D.C.
Bishop Harvey Lewis, Pastor

The Word Sanctified Church
Trenton, NJ
Gail Boyle, Pastor

Tower of Faith Evangelistic Church
Compton, CA
Reuben P. Anderson, Pastor

Trinity All Nations MBC
Memphis, TN
Elder R.E. Berry, Pastor

Union Presbyterian Church
Los Angeles, CA
Phillip Tsuchiya, Pastor

University Ministries International
Tallahassee, FL
Bishop Joseph L. Brown, Pastor

Victory Christian Center
Los Angeles, CA
Elder Prince A. Sykes, Pastor

Victory Harvest COGIC
Santa Maria, CA
Elder Orie Johnson, Pastor

Warren Memorial COGIC
Gary, IN
Dr. W. Lovelle Warren, Sr., Pastor

West Adams Foursquare Church
Los Angeles, CA
Marvin and Juanita Smith, Pastors

West Angeles COGIC
Los Angeles, CA
Bishop Charles E. Blake, Sr., Pastor

West End COGIC
San Antonio, TX
Bishop J.W. Denney, Pastor

White Rose COGIC
Port Arthur, TX
Rev. Wilson Balka, Pastor

Whole Truth Temple COGIC
Los Angeles, CA
Elder D. J. Morgan, Pastor

Worship in Truth COGIC
Rancho Cucamonga, CA
Elder Kevin Moreland, Pastor

Appendix F

Recommended Reading

Prayer

Dabney, Mother E.J. *What it Means to Pray Through*, Church of God in Christ Publishing Board (Memphis, TN), 1987.

Eastman, Dick. *Change the World School of Prayer*, Every Home for Christ (Colorado Springs, CO), 1983.

Garlow Wade, Judy. *Take the Name of Jesus With You: A Practical Guide for Reaching Your Community Through Prayer*, Wesleyan Publishing House (Indianapolis, IN), 2003.

Fasting

Bueno-Aguer, Lee. *Fast Your Way to Health*, Whitaker House (New Kensington, PA), 1991.

Daughtry, Joann Theresa. *Fasting: The Spiritual and the Physical Effects of Fasting*, Disciples on the Move Ministry (Los Angeles, CA), 2000.

Franklin, Jentezen. *Fasting: Opening Doors to a Deeper, More Intimate, More Powerful Relationship With God*, Charisma House-Strang Company (Lake Mary, FL), 2008.

Saxion, Valerie. *How to Feel Great All the Time:* A Lifelong Plan for Unlimited Energy and Radiant Good Health, Bronze Bow Publishing (Minneapolis, MN), 2003.

Shaw, Gwen. *Your Appointment With God: A Bible Study on Fasting*, End-Time Handmaidens (Jasper, AK), 1977.

Physical Benefits of Fasting

Bueno-Aguer, Lee. *Fast Your Way to Health*, Whitaker House (New Kensington, PA), 1991.

Saxion, Valerie. *How to Feel Great All the Time:* A Lifelong Plan for Unlimited Energy and Radiant Good Health, Bronze Bow Publishing (Minneapolis, MN), 2003.

Shelton, Herbert. *Fasting Can Save Your Life*, American Natural Hygiene Society (Tampa, FL), 1978.

CPSIA information can be obtained at www.ICGtesting.com
Printed in the USA
LVOW131945200412

278524LV00001B/1/P